ANTHONY OLIVER

Staffordshire Pottery

The Tribal Art of England

HEINEMANN : LONDON

William Heinemann Ltd
10 Upper Grosvenor Street, London WIX 9PA
LONDON   MELBOURNE   TORONTO
JOHANNESBURG   AUCKLAND

First published 1981

Unless otherwise stated, all photographs,
both black-and-white and colour, are by
courtesy of Oliver-Sutton Antiques, 34c
Kensington Church Street, London W.8.

Printed in Great Britain by
Balding + Mansell, London and Wisbech

Staffordshire Pottery

The Tribal Art of England

Also by Anthony Oliver

The Victorian Staffordshire Figure:
A Guide for Collectors

Fiction
The Pew Group

Contents

Preface

This book is biased. It cannot be otherwise because basically it is a love story and no one loves without prejudice.

Since Sir Herbert Read wrote his book *Staffordshire Pottery Figures* in 1928 there have been many others. Most of them were excellent, the odd one or two were awful; inaccurate and misleading. Nearly all of them, good and bad, are now out of print. The best can still be found on the shelves of our public libraries so that students and collectors can consult them and delve as deeply as they may wish into the history and the family trees of the more famous schools of Staffordshire potters. That ground has been well covered and is not the substance of this book.

By the same token I believe it to be repetitive and unnecessary to embark here upon long technical dissertations on the various types of clay bodies and glazes used by the potters at different periods, except perhaps where this could clarify some interesting point for collectors and add to their fun and enjoyment. Ten years ago when I wrote *The Victorian Staffordshire Figure* I dedicated it with affection to the unknown potters of Staffordshire. Gratifyingly, as I write today it is still in print. I wrote as one who had been a collector for twenty-five years and as a dealer specializing in the pieces I loved best. I am still collecting and in the last ten years, together with my partner Peter Sutton, I have been surrounded by Staffordshire pottery figures for eight hours in every day and for six days of the week. In that time it would be strange if I had not learned something more about them and about my fellow collectors, and it is for them that I have written this book.

Acknowledgements

I suspect that for some authors acknowledgements, like bibliographies, can be a great temptation. How delightfully simple to confer upon oneself the qualities of instant erudition and diligence not to mention the hint of patronage in high places.

Now it so happens that in the preparation of this book I never felt the need to seek permission to consult the Royal Archives at Windsor Castle and upon reflection I regret it. How splendid it could have been to begin this section with a royal fanfare.

"I am deeply indebted to Her Majesty The Queen who graciously allowed me access to her private collection and for her personal kindness and enthusiasm even to dashing up and down library steps to draw my attention to obscure references I might otherwise have missed."

Alas no. Next time perhaps. Mind you I could indeed blow quite a few rather impressive trumpet blasts but then, collectors, be they ever so elevated or famous, do not care to attract the nefarious attention of thieves. It's sad for my acknowledgements but then we live in a sad age.

Museums, however, are – or should be – well protected and fair game and so to the following institutions I am honestly and genuinely indebted and grateful for so many kindnesses over the years: Bodleian Library, Oxford; Brighton Art Gallery and Museum; British Museum and Library; Fitzwilliam Museum, Cambridge; Reference Library, Royal Borough of Kensington and Chelsea; Museum of London; National Maritime Museum; Norwich Castle Museum; Royal Naval Museum, Portsmouth; Salisbury Library; Tate Gallery; National Museum of Wales; The Welsh Folk Museum.

In Staffordshire itself at the City Museum and Art Gallery in Hanley the Director, Mr Arnold Mountford, has always taken great pains to answer my questions most fully, always with his natural courtesy and I thank him. This country is well served by its museums and the dedicated men who run them. It is largely due to Arnold Mountford's foresight that his museum has been able to acquire Admiral Pugh's collection of Staffordshire Portrait Figures, one of the finest collections in the world. There could be no better or more fitting home for it.

In the London Library the Librarian, Mr Douglas Matthews, has always been most kind and helpful as indeed have all the staff there. Here in particular I want to thank Miss Joan Bailey who must have saved me many hours' work by her unfailingly cheerful efforts on my behalf and her encyclopaedic knowledge of the catalogues and shelves of that most remarkable of libraries.

I am especially indebted to the many learned collectors who have shared their enthusiasm and friendship with me. I am grateful for their loyalty and trust. In particular to Mr and Mrs G. Barnett for the photograph of the rare and beautiful group in Figure 226; Mr and Mrs Edward Behar; Mr David Crane who took the trouble to photograph items for me from his ancillary collection of theatre prints; Mr Reginald Haggar who kindly gave me permission to quote from his book *Staffordshire Chimney Ornaments*; Miss Mary Honeywood who most generously allowed me full access to her notes and illustrations on rural workers and their costumes in nineteenth century England and Wales and for her constant kindness and encouragement; Captain K. J. Douglas-Morris D.L. Royal Navy for his very specialized knowledge and research so cheerfully undertaken on my behalf; Mr Parry Michael, Staffordshire collector extraordinary, whose scholarship and sense of humour have often enlightened and delighted me whenever I have sought his aid. Rear Admiral P. D. G. Pugh has, as always, been generous with his specialized knowledge, for that and for his friendship I am grateful. So much kindness indeed from so many collectors both in this country and scattered all over the world that I hope they will understand and forgive me if I do not name them all.

To Messrs Christie Manson and Woods and Messrs Sotheby Parke Bernet both in London and New York my thanks are due, also to *Art and Antiques Weekly* and to *The Antique Collector and Collector's Guide*.

At William Heinemann, my publishers, everyone has been very kind and helpful; in particular, Mr Peter Ireland and Miss Julia Nash have given me a great deal of practical and expert help and I thank them sincerely as I do Mr Michael Horniman of A. P. Watt Ltd. for the same reasons.

Mr Timothy Manderson is not only my publisher but my trusted guide and mentor in all my writing. In his friendship and that of his wife Carol I count myself among the most fortunate of authors.

It takes time to write a book and without the most generous of business partners it would not have been possible. I have therefore left my thanks to Mr Peter Sutton to the last. I thank him now not only for the extra work he has unselfishly and cheerfully undertaken on my behalf but for his wise and scholarly advice upon which I have so often relied during the preparation and writing of this book, and it is to him I owe my greatest debt.

ANTHONY OLIVER
February 1981

List of Colour Plates

Note Heights of all Staffordshire figures can vary slightly.

1. A typical Pew Group, very rare, Staffordshire salt-glaze. *c.*1740. 6½ ins. Crown copyright Victoria and Albert Museum.

The Eighteenth Century

There's no doubt about it, Staffordshire pottery is uncompromising. It does not mix well with the sophisticated elegance of porcelain. And yet at once this needs qualifying because much of the naïve output of our potters was made in porcelain. It is the style more than the chemical nature of the figures which is incompatible.

Some years ago in a small country auction we bought a mixed lot of figures. They were all Staffordshire except for one little figure of a girl playing a hurdy-gurdy and she, poor love, was hard paste porcelain. German most likely and about 1860. Since we had not counted her in the value of the lot I stuck a cheap price on her and put her on the shelves with the others hoping to tempt someone for a quick sale. It wasn't any good, no one took any notice of her. Of course, most of the people who visit the shop are Staffordshire collectors but even those among them who were beginners with little knowledge showed not the slightest interest in her. So obvious was the difference in style that they felt instinctively she was out of place. In the end I gave the poor thing to a church jumble-sale where I hope she found someone to take pity on her.

It is almost as if the contents of the shop were acting in the capacity of a censor and dictating what shall be allowed to share it with them. In a way that is true, and since most of the things I love are of the nineteenth century, and of those the greater number Victorian, it is interesting to note over the years the things which will appear acceptable when displayed with them.

Earlier English pottery made in Staffordshire marries very well and lives quite happily alongside the later period. It prefers a section of its own but it doesn't look out of place. Underglaze printed pottery, pot lids and similar ware, fits in too but so curiously enough does the marble-like product of parian porcelain.

Long before the happy vulgarity of the Victorian period caught the imagination of collectors there was great interest in the products of the earlier years. Even before the First World War collectors were drawn to the pottery made in Staffordshire in the eighteenth century and earlier. Pick up some of those old magazines and books on antiques nowadays and you might as well be reading the catalogue of a museum. Of course the same thing will happen in the future and collectors will read wistfully of the fine and rare Victorian pieces which are still available to us today. So does this mean that we cannot hope to collect any earlier than the Victorian period? My experience tells me that this is not so if you know what to look for.

The very first Staffordshire pottery figures and groups, as opposed to the more ordinary output of plates, mugs and other useful kitchen wares, began to appear in the early years of the eighteenth century, round about 1720–40. They were charming little naïve pieces with a body of white salt-glazed stoneware; but unless you are rich you can forget them. And the same sadly applies to the delightful little primitive figures attributed to John Astbury and Thomas Whieldon. Since I hope and intend this book to be of practical use to the collector of the 1980s there seems little point in describing rare figures which are far beyond the means of most of us and in covering ground which has been exhaustively explored by others before me. Like the early salt-glaze figures most of those attributed to Astbury and Whieldon have gone to the great museum collections, notably the Fitzwilliam Museum in Cambridge and the Burnap Collection in Kansas City in America. Not many have remained in private collections and when occasionally they do appear in sale-rooms they fetch a great deal of money. Typical of this earliest period are the so-called Pew Groups in white salt-glazed stoneware. (1) They all look a bit alike, usually two men in contemporary eighteenth century dress seated on either side of a woman on a high-backed settle or pew. I suppose there can be no more than twenty of them surviving which is why they command such high prices.

I remember wandering around the stalls of a church fête in Suffolk some time ago. It was a bright sunny day and the stalls were laid out in the grounds of a private house. There were the usual games of hoop-la and warm ladies glowing with perspiration and Christian spirit cajoling visitors to guess the number of currants in a cake. The lawn sloped down to a low boundary wall with a few trees bent permanently by the winter gales blowing in from the sea which on that day was blue and calm in the distance. Near the wall was a stall covered in second-hand bits and pieces, electric irons, brass ash-trays and a jumble of old bits of china and pottery. It was a most glorious day, the sort of day usually reserved for memories of childhood, warm and happy and full of promise. As I walked towards the stall I saw a patch of white pottery gleaming in the sunshine half buried in the jumble of pots and pans. Although I was some distance away, too far to see any close detail, it seemed almost as though I had been suddenly blessed with telescopic sight. Today, if ever, I thought, will be the day when I found a Pew Group on a Bring and Buy stall in a village fête. Only an elderly lady was approaching the stall ahead of me and I had to walk very quickly to pass her. No one likes the idea of physical combat with an old lady, armed as she was with a walking stick, so I quickened my pace and beat her to the prize by a short head.

No, it wasn't a Pew Group. Only a sad white gardening glove with three fingers sitting up demurely on a pew settle formed by the palm of the glove. We all do it of course, it is part of the excitement and joy of collecting and it *could* have happened; who knows it still might one day. I often thought about that lovely day in an English garden and later on I wrote a novel and called it *The Pew Group*, so the day wasn't wasted completely. (1)

So then, Pew Groups and the later figures of the eighteenth century attributed to potters like Astbury and Whieldon (2, 3) are not for us. I mention them only because

2

2. Water Buffalo showing Chinese influence, tortoise-shell glaze. School of Thomas Whieldon. *c.*1750. 7¾ ins. Crown copyright Victoria and Albert Museum.

3. A Whieldon figure of a Suffolk Punch horse, tortoise-shell and ochre streaked glaze, translucent green base. *c.*1760. 7¼ ins.

4. Gardener and girl. Ralph Wood, coloured glaze. *c.*1775. 8 ins.

5. Toby Jug with tortoise-shell glaze more typical of Whieldon than Wood. *c.*1770. 10 ins.

they are the beginning of the story, because they are full of quiet humour and because they share many qualities with the later figures which are more accessible to the ordinary collector today. The only other thing worth noting about the early figures before we leave them in their museums is that the whole period is sadly lacking in documentation of any kind. Through the years the barest scraps of gossip and guesswork have come to be accepted if not as proven fact then as a useful shorthand for collectors and sale-room catalogues. You may if you please read all the many good and learned books on this early period with pleasure but not much profit; I don't think it's very important anyway. The figures remain and speak for themselves as it was always intended they should.

Shortly after this early salt-glaze period of doubts and uncertainties the scene becomes quite a lot clearer when the family of potters called Wood began to make their mark. Quite literally so because they were the first Staffordshire potters to use marks; and figures by them variously impressed R. WOOD, Ra. Wood; Ra. Wood, Burslem, or

4

more rarely a rebus mark depicting trees, quite often appear in sale-rooms and in antique shops. Well, perhaps not quite often but enough to make it possible to add to a modest collection. I realize that if this book is to be of some practical use to a collector then such a vague word as modest simply will not do. How modest? Bank clerk, company director, nurse or student? And yet the moment hard figures of money are mentioned in a book you can encounter the most formidable difficulties. To do so in an age of inflation such as ours could well be the reverse of helpful and only lead collectors to disappointment and confusion. Current television programmes on antiques and their market value are invariably followed by a special announcement explaining how in a few short months since the programme was recorded, the experts' estimates must be discounted because the price of silver and gold has trebled. Special books with price guides are published with loose leaf supplements inserted which are themselves often out-of-date by the time the book appears in the shops. Sale-rooms often supply a list of estimated prices as a guide for prospective bidders which frequently prove to be too low and sometimes mercifully too high.

So what is the best advice for a collector who is interested in Staffordshire pottery and wants to buy pieces that will give him pleasure without spending a fortune and without buying rubbish? It might be thought that as a dealer my advice to consult a dealer might be regarded with a certain amount of reserve, and yet I do so because I believe it passionately to be good advice. For many years before I became a dealer I was an avid and consistent collector and it is because I can remember all the doubts and difficulties that I suffered then when I was learning the hard way that I can best help collectors now.

Sale-rooms are the great clearing houses of the antique trade. They perform a valuable and necessary service and on the whole they do it extremely well. I know that many dealers and collectors have complained bitterly about what they believe to be severe shortcomings in the system of public auction with all the advantages seeming to be heavily weighted in favour of the sale-rooms and almost none of their rules of procedure acting to the advantage of the buyer. These complaints, I believe, arise because of a fundamental misconception of the service one has a right to expect from a sale-room. They are not philanthropic institutions. Their primary purpose is to make money for themselves and for their shareholders and a quick glance at their published company reports and profits will prove conclusively that they do this supremely well. A dealer, too, is concerned to make a profit but his function is quite different from that of the sale-room. His relationship with his collectors is blessed with the great luxury of allowing them to decide at leisure and to guide their choosing with expert and personal advice. At auction the buyer must commit himself in seconds. With a dealer with whom he has established a relationship of mutual trust he may well consider the next addition to his collection over a period of days or sometimes even weeks.

I've wandered away from the work of the Wood family of Burslem but I'll come back to them later. The truth is I'm not very fond of them.

For a collector, especially a beginner, the great problem with sale-rooms is indeed time. Very often a collector will only be able to get to the sale-room on the day of the sale itself when he will find that the lots to be sold may only be viewed for a few rushed moments, if indeed he is allowed to handle them at all. You can't blame the sale-rooms, they may have many hundreds of lots to sell and you really cannot expect them to hold up the day's business while hoards of collectors try and decide which figure was made in 1820 and which is the later copy of 1890, and which, if either, has been repaired or restored (by no means all catalogues specify condition, the bidder is left to assess it for himself).

For most sales the lots can be viewed in much more comfort two or three days before the auction. It's worth while finding out before you go whether you will need a special permit to view. There have been quite a few thefts on viewing days and some sale-rooms sensibly safeguard themselves by issuing such permits after references have been submitted and ask viewers to sign a book with their name and address. Almost all of them protect the sale goods in locked glass cabinets.

Now it might be thought that all these precautions are designed specifically to make life extraordinarily complicated for the prospective buyer and so far I haven't even mentioned the sale itself. In fact they are quite sensible rules formulated through years of experience to facilitate the smooth running of the daily traffic in the sale-room so that it can present and sell to the bidders the greatest number of accurately catalogued lots within an allotted period of time. I say, accurately, although of course mistakes do occur in catalogues and the wonder is not that they do but that there are comparatively few of them.

Just consider for a moment the enormous number of lots handled by a sale-room, sometimes thousands every week, every one of which must be described and specified in a few lines of print. I imagine that the cataloguer dictates to a trusty secretary who faithfully records every word. Not long ago a collector telephoned me from Northern Ireland.

"I'm coming to London next week so if you have any Staffordshire birds do put them on one side and I'll come and see you in your shop. I'm coming over for a Christie's pottery sale just for one lot, a starling."

"Christie's sale next week?"

"That's right, sounds very interesting. I haven't got a starling."

"Funny, I've viewed that sale and I can't remember a Staffordshire starling."

"Lot 309, a grey starling in a boat, I'd like that."

"Look, you'd better let me check and I'll ring you back."

It was just as well I did for his "grey starling in a boat", so clearly printed in the catalogue, turned out to be a Staffordshire portrait group of the lifeboat heroine Grace Darling and she wouldn't have fitted into his collection at all. At least he was able to save the cost of his journey.

Thirty years ago as a collector I made some expensive mistakes in sale-rooms before I learned how to use my eyes carefully and spot the restored figures and the late reproductions which were not so well known then. They still creep into the sale-rooms, not so often in London, but some country sale-rooms are stacked with them. When a collector has knowledge and knows what he is buying, sale-rooms can be exciting and rewarding but for a beginner it's like fiddling about inside a television set with wet hands.

Later on I'll talk about a sale and try to be as helpful as I can. What I'm saying now is that the new collector will be far better off consulting a specialist dealer, asking his advice, and listening and learning before plunging in to buy a pig in a poke.

Back to the Woods. Ralph Wood (1715–72) and his son Ralph Wood Junior (1748–95) worked so closely together that no one is absolutely certain which of them made what. It doesn't matter a great deal for their figures are very much alike, as you might expect. There is a current theory that the father produced less than he has hitherto been credited with and that the majority of the figures were in fact the work of his son. If you like them and you want to study the subject deeply you can do no better than to read Frank Falkner's splendid book, *The Wood Family of Burslem*. It was written way back in 1912 but any good library should have a copy.

The single technical feature which distinguishes the work of the Woods is their use of coloured glazes. Instead of painting the unfired figure with metallic oxides and then dipping the entire piece into a transparent glaze solution, they added the colouring oxide to the liquid glaze itself so that the decorator would have perhaps four or five pots of glaze each containing a different oxide, and thus the figures were painted and glazed in a single operation. When fired, the colours would be inside the glaze like a stained glass window: clear, lustrous and transparent. Often the painters of Wood's figures seem to have made little or no serious attempt to confine any one colour to a specific area. Green, black, grey, brown, purple and variations of these shades where the glazes flowed into each other ran genteel riot over a Ralph Wood figure. The general effect may be fairly and accurately described as wishy-washy. Later figures from the factory used many of the earlier moulds but were decorated with enamel colours fired on over the glaze.

I don't really know why I dislike Wood figures. Technically, as we have seen, they were innovative and the quality of the block making and moulding was considerably higher than in any other Staffordshire pottery figures which had gone before. In my youth, and indeed many years before I was born, they were greatly admired and always fetched good prices. Comparing the true value of money today they have obviously fallen in value and I can only suppose their lack of attraction for the modern eye is responsible.

They were never a true folk art and their attempt to appeal to the sophisticated aristocratic taste which was being promoted by Josiah Wedgwood at his Etruria factory resulted in a flood of classical subjects all with very similarly moulded faces. A group of Ralph Wood figures can look depressingly like the out-patients department of a hyperthyroid clinic. Even their animals have the unmistakable Wood stamp on their faces so that lions, stags and sheep bear a distinct likeness to vicars, shepherdesses and flute players.

Ralph Wood Senior is suspected of having invented and of producing the first Toby Jugs. It is a serious accusation and although not proved beyond doubt I wouldn't put it past him. I said some very rude things indeed about Toby Jugs in my first book but I must admit it has not prevented a devoted band of faithful collectors from pursuing them with dogged determination whenever they appear. This continuing interest probably explains why they have come closer to holding their value than the nymph and shepherd brigade. (6)

If my purely personal prejudice hasn't dented your loyalty and you like Ralph Wood figures enough to collect them, I can at least give you some practical hints.

Restoration

A very high proportion of Ralph Wood figures have been restored, so be careful. Early restoration is easy to spot because the paint covering the repair will have discoloured. Some modern restoration work is wonderfully clever and can easily be missed. Nevertheless it is still restoration and the new glaze will not be remotely the same composition as the coloured glazes of Ralph Wood, it will only appear to be so. A specialist dealer should certainly know if a figure has been restored and will be happy to say so on your receipt. Unless it is grossly and extensively restored don't let it put you off.

Mould

A figure will vary considerably in crispness depending upon how early or late it came from the mould. Look for those hyperthyroid eyes, the bulge of the eyeball should be sharply delineated by a clearly moulded upper and lower eye lid. If the eyes are sharp it's a good early mould and the other details on the figure will be good too. It's a quick, simple check.

Some figures are covered over and glazed on the under surface of the base, some are hollow and unglazed inside. By no means all of them bear one of the factory marks but I will say this for them; Wood figures are so very distinctive in style that they do not need a mark to identify them. Sometimes a figure bears an impressed number on the base, Falkner notes a series from 1 to 169 of which he lists a description of 83, and others have been identified since. In the early twentieth century when they were very popular there

6. Shepherd and Shepherdess, coloured glaze, impressed mark Ra Wood Burslem. *c.*1775. 11 ins.

7. Bull-baiting. Ralph Wood coloured glaze. *c.*1785. 6¾ ins.

9

8. Admiral Van Tromp and Venus with Cupid. Ralph Wood
coloured glazes. *c.*1775. The bases are both typical of the factory.
$10\frac{1}{2}$, $10\frac{3}{4}$ ins.

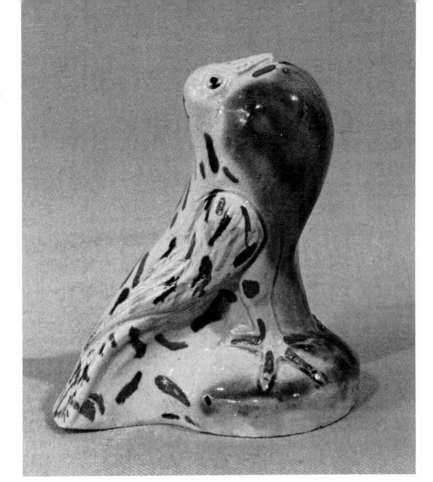

9. "The Norwich Cropper". Prattware pouter pigeon. c.1796. $4\frac{1}{8}$ ins.

were some attempts at forgeries but they were very crude and a modern attempt I have seen, a figure of Old Age, is also very poor.

Far more figures were produced by the Woods than by any other Staffordshire potters of the eighteenth century and good examples of their work may still be found at reasonable prices. They are not much to my taste, as you will have guessed, but their quality and workmanship is undeniable and to my mind they are today underpriced. (6, 7, 8)

There is another distinctive and interesting group of figures which appeared in Staffordshire towards the end of the eighteenth century and continued in production well into the reign of Victoria. They are generally called Pratt-ware because, by tradition, some of them have been attributed to William Pratt, a potter of Lane Delph. Some Pratt-type figures are quite crude but others are exceptionally well modelled, rivalling and surpassing similar figures made by Ralph Wood. All of them share a distinctive range of high-temperature-proof colours which allowed them to be fired beneath the glaze. Not in the glaze like the early Woods, nor over it like Walton and Sherratt, but underneath it.

10. Pratt-ware Lion. *c.*1790. 12 ins.

11. Titled Jupiter in underglaze blue, cursive script beneath the base. Pratt-ware. *c.*1775. $15\frac{1}{4}$ ins.

Once seen these colours are unmistakable; a browny purple with various shades of yellow, orange-ochre and a drab sage green with often quite large passages of a pale cobalt blue. (9, 10, 11)

Some jugs were impressed PRATT but I have never seen a figure so marked and the truth is that the type was made by so many different potters that it is impossible now to decide who made what. That isn't important but as a dealer I know that some very fine figures of the Pratt-type may still be found. They are refreshingly bright and cheerful and good examples would enhance any collection.

~ 2 ~
Late Eighteenth and
Early Nineteenth Centuries

It may seem an odd thing for me to say but I believe there are too many books about pottery. Well, too many books of a certain kind anyway. Pedantry is your great killer of enthusiasm and all too often a printed family tree of potters, a list of factory addresses, or an entry from a church register can so confuse and discourage a new collector as to send him spinning into ceramic circles where he won't know his Astbury from his Whieldon.

A collector begins his obsession by seeing some figures that arouse his interest. If he is lucky he will find more of them and his interest will turn to love before some book fusses him with the information that the potter married twice, that the second wife signed the marriage register with a cross and that there is in any case some considerable doubt that we have got hold of the right potter in the first place. Great chunks of many a learned tome could be excised without any loss in research and a considerable gain in appreciation. It is all very like the famous medical lecture, a perfect example of honesty and brevity:

> "This morning, gentlemen, we shall consider the
> spleen. About the spleen, gentlemen, we know
> nothing. So much for the spleen."

I am not saying that research cannot be the most absorbing and rewarding pursuit. I have spent too many hours in that happy occupation to believe anything so foolish. What I do say is that research and study is a luxury a collector should, at the beginning of his obsession, treat with caution and reserve, otherwise he may well not see the Wood for the family tree. Later on it can be enormous fun and add a great deal to the pleasure of collecting, but in the early days it should be the pots he studies and not the potters. And the best way to study the pots is to handle them and look at them carefully.

Not only the Woods flourished in the last quarter of the eighteenth century. A whole host of splendid figures poured out of the Staffordshire potteries at that time and many of them are much neglected by today's collectors. A surprising number of those potters signed their work, far more than did so in the ceramic explosion of the Victorian period. A marked figure will always cost more than its unsigned contemporary but a new collector who is attracted to the period should consider the money well spent. A marked piece is a touchstone, a constant and irrefutable reference for comparison and appreciation. Soon, without so much as a glance at a family tree, the figure will speak

12. The four seasons of the year. Typical fine quality pottery figures of this factory, impressed mark Neale & Co. c.1780. 5⅜ ins. By courtesy of the Fitzwilliam Museum, Cambridge.

for itself. I don't know why there are more figures without a factory mark than with one but it is so. It does, however, make it very satisfying to be able to compare figures and to be able to see clearly that they come without a shadow of doubt from the same hand. Well, to be honest, you can't always do that but in a gratifyingly high percentage of cases you can.

Who was working at that time and producing marked figures worth considering and which are today within a price range which won't bankrupt you? James Neale for one. Don't, I beg you, fly to a reference book and look him up yet. Later if you like, but to begin with it is enough to know his name. For collectors the figures are more important than the man. It is enough to know his dates (1740–1814) and that his taste effectively imposed a style upon the figures which came from his factory over a period of years. Neale or Neale & Co in impressed capitals or lower case letters and sometimes a crown over the letter G are clearly marked on some of the most delicate and finely potted figures to have been made in Staffordshire. In some ways Neale's work stands alone in excellence and quality. When you first see them you may well find it difficult to believe that they are indeed pottery and not porcelain. Many of his figures are quite small, about 5 inches high, and stand on a distinctive rococo base over a simple stepped rectangular or square foot which is decorated with a plain single line that varies in colour from a deep purple-crimson to a lighter shade of pink. The moulds are

14

13. The Assassination of Jean Paul
Marat, impressed Lakin & Poole. *c.*1793.
13¾ ins. By courtesy of the City Museum,
Stoke-on-Trent.

wonderfully clean cut and sharp and show evidence of considerable finishing by hand.
The glaze is always bright, clear and lustrous and as much as any other feature of
Neale's work is responsible for their close resemblance to the delicacy of porcelain.
They are quite as distinctive in their individual style as Ralph Wood figures but their
small, sprigged flower patterns in fresh enamel colours could never be mistaken for the
work of the early Wood period. (12)

Once you have a marked Neale figure you will be able with a high degree of accuracy
to identify other examples of his work and there are more of them available at
reasonable prices than is generally supposed. Handle, look closely, use your eyes; those
are the simple secrets of collecting unmarked figures. Don't let your eyes record lazily,
don't accept a simple sprig of flowers as just another eighteenth century example of the
decorator's art. How many petals are there? How many sprays of miniature leaves?
Look very closely at the enamel colour and the thickness of the individual brush strokes.
Remember that these figures were made in their hundreds of thousands and that
decorators working for a long period of time would almost inevitably reproduce their
patterns by hand in such a distinctively individual style as to identify the figure just as
certainly as if it bore the impressed factory mark itself. Like the Ralph Woods, Neale's
work I believe to be at present somewhat neglected and under-valued. He had been
originally a selling agent in London for Humphrey Palmer, a potter who imitated the
jasper wares of Wedgwood. He took over Palmer's works in 1776 when he went bank-

rupt but Neale's figures were quite different from that marmoreal school of potters.

There are other factories that marked figures, but to be practical I don't advise anyone to try and make a collection because not enough of them turn up to make it worth while. Lakin and Poole for example (impressed mark in capital letters) only operated effectively from 1791–5 and I almost never see them. (13) Of course, you may well consider it worth while to try and secure as many single examples of marked figures of different factories from the latter part of the century and for that matter on into the early years of the nineteenth. I've often thought that if I were starting as a collector and not so faithfully committed to my beloved anonymous Victorians, it would be an interesting and fascinating collection to make.

I have collectors who specialize in specific factories, and collectors whose self imposed restrictions are a source of endless wonder to me. Collectors for sheep, cows, sailors, flags, rural pastimes, dragons, dragoons, dolphins, dairymaids, unicorns, acorns, ships, watermills and many many more curious categories all of which they manage to find in one form or another, caught and handed down to them by the ingenuity and imagination of those amazing men in the potteries of Staffordshire. But strangely I have no one who specializes in making a collection of as many different factory marked specimens as may come their way. It could make a most interesting and even important collection with a lot to commend it. There would be perhaps marginally less competition with other collectors; after all, once you had your Neale or your Lakin and Poole you could relax. Collectors can be quite ruthless in pursuit of quarry. I have seen two of them in my shop both firmly clutching a figure and refusing to release it. What did I do? I chose between them, that's what I did. I reckoned that the tweed skirt had beaten the silk headscarf by two tenths of a second and so I lost the custom of the headscarf forever, which was sad because dealers collect collectors.

Such a collection would also mean a good deal of peace of mind for a beginner. A marked figure from a minor potter is unlikely to be faked. Too much trouble for a modern forger to simulate the quality of Neale even if he could, but take care. I did say minor, meaning a potter whose output was comparatively small. It is a different matter when a potter with a vast production like John Walton is considered. There are many pieces on the market impressed with a fair imitation of his mark and one or two of them have succeeded so well that they may be seen boldly illustrated as genuine examples in more than one book on Staffordshire pottery. (14, 15)

Perhaps this is the right place to consider the work of Walton. He was so prolific that he is one of the few potters genuine examples of whose work may still be found in some of the most modest of country antique shops. At first thought it may seem surprising that anyone should bother to fake Walton but if we give it a little more consideration we shall see that it must be quite a lucrative venture.

With Walton we leave the eighteenth century and can consider the first quarter of the nineteenth and the years leading up to the accession of Victoria in 1837. He seems

14. A modern reproduction bearing an imitation of the impressed mark of John Walton. Such figures have frequently appeared in sale-rooms and sold as genuine. $c.1970.$ $6\frac{3}{4}$ ins.

15. The tower on the left bears a genuine Walton mark in Roman capitals. The fake mark of the figure on the right is poorly impressed and in plain capitals. $c.1820,$ $c.1970.$ $5\frac{1}{2}$, $6\frac{3}{4}$ ins.

to have been producing figures from about 1806 to 1835. Watching the market trend closely I believe this period to be at present much neglected by collectors and that because of this prices for figures by Walton and his many contemporary imitators are unnaturally depressed. Of the man himself we know almost nothing. He had a factory in Navigation Road, Burslem, and made distinctive figures and groups, almost always with a stylized leafy tree or bocage at the back. He seems to have used his mark more than anyone else since the Woods, and you can find his name impressed in capital letters about a quarter of an inch high enclosed in a slightly undulating scroll at the back of many of his pieces or more rarely underneath. A single impressed capital W is also attributed with less certainty to him but it would seem more likely that figures so marked are from one of the Wood family.

There has been a tendency to dismiss Walton as a potter of rather crudely modelled rural and religious figures; charming rather than accomplished. In fact he was capable of work of great merit and his best pieces are well worth searching for and collecting. Have a look for the quality that you can see clearly in Figures 16 and 17. Walton's version of a religious theme which appears in many other potters' work but never better than this example of the Flight into Egypt. The modelling is superb; imaginative without strain and although you can see the influence of the Wood school the faces, and indeed the whole conception of the group, are a decided improvement on their usual rather po-faced immobility.

There is some evidence that Walton in his early work may have followed the Wood technique of using stained glazes, but the vast majority of his figures are coloured with enamels applied on top of the glaze and fired lightly again so that they set and sank into it in a satisfying range of colours, most notably a bright singing apple green. Singing is a good word for Walton, both for his colours and his figures. He escaped from the dead hand of the eighteenth century Neo-Classicism and sang out a brighter more cheerful tune. The simple songs of the countryside and the pub, rather than the pretentious tinklings played laboriously on a parlour piano by a *nouveau riche* farmer's daughter prodded into the classics by the artificially high profits on corn.

That is the true significance of Walton. He was one of the first potters to turn his back on the gentilities of the late eighteenth century. He preferred the world about him to a world of myths and legends. His farmers and their women were working in real fields only a few miles from his factory in Burslem, not floating around in diaphanous draperies among the meadows of Elysium.

If in this modern age we have so lost our faith that we count religion as a myth or a legend we must remember that for Walton it wasn't so. His saints and prophets were as real to him as his sheep and his cows, and the crucifixion a pledge of faith and hope for a better world. (18)

Walton is a great bridge between the two centuries. Between a world where children however poor at least could breathe fresh air, and a world where they worked in the

16. The Flight into Egypt,
Walton. c.1815. 10¼ ins.

17. Another
version with its
pair, both
impressed Walton.
c.1820. 7¼ ins.

18. The naïve and primitive quality of Walton's crucifixion somehow makes its message immediate, real and infinitely moving. Like being told the story for the first time by a child. *c*.1815. 10½ ins.

factories for twelve hours a day and died of lead poisoning before they were thirty. Within this period which takes us up to Victoria's accession, the boundaries of the small towns in Staffordshire had expanded until eventually they would merge into the huge industrial conglomerate we call the Potteries. The green fields became a memory in the new slums all over England, a memory kept alive and saluted by Walton's mantel-shelf meadows where sheep still grazed and his brave bocage the only thing left which was fresh and green; a symbol of hope in a world where the water was poisoned by sewage and the air thick with smoke and lead.

This same bocage will repay handsomely the time any collector cares to give it. A

19. Sherratt bocage on his version of The Flight into Egypt.

20. Unusual bocage found on some Walton figures. It is this bocage which has been crudely imitated in Figure 14.

21. Walton.

22. Walton reverse view.

glance at Figures 19–27 show some of the various types of leaf modelling favoured by early nineteenth century Staffordshire pieces. The fun comes from matching bocage from pieces signed with a potter's mark to unmarked pieces. If they bear a strong similarity, the pieces may show other features which tally so closely as to make possible a definite assumption that they are from the same factory.

Bocage alone is not enough because plagiarism was common in the potteries and Walton's work was copied by many of his contemporaries. His most favoured type of bocage was a stylized oak leaf arranged symmetrically in a cluster of five or six, sometimes with an acorn in the centre or more often a brightly coloured flower with six or eight petals. (28–31)

Walton himself was not the originator of bocage, it derives from the earlier porcelain of Chelsea and Derby and Bow. What Walton did was to simplify and free the style from the rather prissy prettiness of porcelain and transform it into a bold naïve design more suited to pottery. So successful was he that at least two other potters, Ralph Hall and Ralph Salt, copied his design exactly. Figures by them impressed Hall or Salt turn

23. Bocage on figure impressed Hall.

24. Another cruder bocage by Hall.

25. Another type of Sherratt bocage.

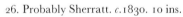

26. Probably Sherratt. c.1830. 10 ins.

27. An unusual form of bocage used as an arbour. Possibly Sherratt, unmarked, but figures of Dr Syntax impressed Salt have been noted. c.1820 8½ ins.

up from time to time but with rare exceptions their quality is poor. Work of an exceedingly high standard in Walton's style has been seen impressed J. Dale Burslem. It equals and even surpasses Walton's finest quality but sadly it is very rare. I once had a brilliant example of his work (32,33) and remember it still with affection and pleasure. No point, then, in searching for John Dale but be thankful that John Walton was more prolific and still well within reach of collectors today.

What should you look for in a good Walton figure? I suppose the great advantage a dealer has in guiding collectors is the enormous number of examples which pass through his hands. They pass through sale-rooms too, but auctioneers don't sit in the same room with them day after day as we do in the shop.

First look at the composition as a whole. It may seem an obvious thing to ask but it is very important. Do you like it? Does the subject and the composition please you? Don't be influenced by the fact that it has a beautifully crisp Walton mark impressed on it. If

28. A delightful Walton study of travelling musicians with a troupe of performing dogs. *c.*1815. 10 ins.

29. All these figures are impressed
Walton. c.1810, c.1815, c.1815. 3½, 7,
5¼ ins.

30. A base rather like a squashed
meringue is often found on Walton pieces.
This one has an interesting detail where
he has used some bocage flowers as
additional decoration. c.1810. 5¾ ins.

31. Lady Archer and companion Hunter.
Such figures were made and impressed by
both Salt and Walton and it is not easy to
decide which of them made these. c.1820. 5¾,
6 ins.

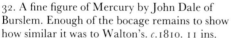

32. A fine figure of Mercury by John Dale of Burslem. Enough of the bocage remains to show how similar it was to Walton's. c.1810. 11 ins.

33. The impressed mark of John Dale Burslem just below Mercury's foot.

it doesn't appeal to you in the shop you are not likely to love it more at home so don't let a dealer persuade you against your inclination.

Look for crispness in the modelling; the faces and the bocage leaves. Look at any painted sprig of floral decoration on skirts or waistcoats. Is it fine and delicate with firm sure brush strokes or does it show signs of having been decorated the morning after the night before? (By no means an uncommon occurrence in some of Walton's pieces.) Is the glaze underneath the base a good strong lead glaze with a hint of pale blue or green? Some Walton pieces, it is true, do have a whiter base glaze but all modern Walton fakes do, so you should be wary of them.

Don't worry about minor damage or repairs. Nearly all bocage has been chipped through the years, it is almost inevitable because of its exposed vulnerability. And don't worry if some of the enamel colour has flaked away unless the amount missing makes the piece look too unattractive to be acceptable. Minor flaking occurs too often for it to affect the value of an otherwise good example and a good dealer will be happy to point out any chips or restoration. Watch out for small figures which may be missing completely. Walton was fond of dotting his pieces with miniature figures, small animals, sheep or dogs. If they have been broken some unscrupulous restorers find it less bother to remove them completely rather than take the trouble to give the creatures new ears or tails. They grind the poor little beast right down to the base and either disguise the missing piece with a clump of fine grass threads made from clay squeezed out like tiny spaghetti, or they simply paint over the grind mark. To be fair to the honourable profession of restorers I have to say that I believe most of such improper surgery to be the work of that great army of little old ladies who have taken up "restoring" in their retirement instead of knitting. I'm told there exist special courses where they are – doubtless for a large fee – actively encouraged in such irresponsible behaviour and I heartily wish they wouldn't do it. I would not complain so much if their caggy-handed enthusiasm were confined to "improving" their private possessions and even less if they were content to replace handles on teacups or stick saucers together, but to encourage the ignorant to cull fictile flocks or to inflict infanticide upon the Widow of Zarephat comes perilously close to condoning vandalism.

There were other potters working in this early part of the nineteenth century who sometimes used a factory mark. Enoch Wood, a cousin and nephew of the two Ralphs is well worth looking for. He worked for his cousin and then on his own or in partnership with a potter called James Caldwell and finally with his own sons. He used enamel colours over the glaze and although his work lacks the fresh originality of Walton, he was less bound to the Neo-Classical theme than his uncle and cousin. His name in various forms and combinations impressed, printed and incised appears on figures often enough to make them available to collectors without costing a fortune.

I think that without any doubt his best periods were his partnership with Caldwell from 1790 to 1818 and subsequently with his sons up to 1840. His famous bust of John Wesley was earlier, about 1781, but unless you are an ardent Methodist I would advise caution before buying a Wesley bust. It was so popular that it was copied by many other potters and some very late examples have appeared complete with a copy of Enoch Wood's original medallion mark impressed at the back. If you really want one badly, get a guaranteed original from a good dealer but don't trust Wesley on his own. Best of all I love Enoch Wood's figures of the comedian John Liston in some of his most famous parts. If you wanted an example of his work at its greatest then a Liston figure is worth searching for. Liston as Lubin Log, as Paul Pry, as Sam Swipes and as Van Dunder have been noted with Wood's impressed mark and a number 15 painted in grey or black near it under the base. I'm not certain of the significance of the painted number but when it sometimes appears on its own and the modelling is up to Enoch Wood's clear, sharp-cut quality I would accept it as proof of his work. There are many other contemporary unmarked Staffordshire versions of these figures, especially of

34. John Liston one of the most famous of all English comedians in two of his roles. As
Sam Swipes in *Exchange No Robbery* and as Van Dunder in '*T'would Puzzle a Conjurer*, by
Enoch Wood and Sons. *c*.1826, *c*.1826. 6¼, 7 ins.

Lubin Log and Paul Pry, but enough examples of Enoch Wood's figures turn up to make them worth waiting for. (34)

As a collector you might well consider all these potters as a practical possibility not too far outside the range of reasonable investment. They are only a very few of the hundreds of potters working in this area in the first quarter of the nineteenth century. I have selected them not solely for their merit but because they are among the minority of factories that chose to identify their figures with a mark. There has never been such a concentration of working potters to compare with the district of North Staffordshire at any time anywhere else in the world and that is probably as true today as it was in the eighteenth and nineteenth centuries. In 1840 the townships and parishes of Stoke-on-Trent, Longton, Fenton, Burslem, Lane Delph, Hanley, Shelton, Cobridge, Longport and Tunstall were still separated by fields and winding lanes with a total population of some 70,000 people; nearly all of them, men, women and children from the age of seven, engaged in the manufacture of pottery and porcelain. (See Chapter 2, *The Victorian Staffordshire Figure.*)

That incredible concentration of potters in an area extending from north to south for nine miles and about three miles wide was totally concerned to supply their fellow countrymen, and a great number of other people all over the world, with every conceivable object which could be manufactured in clay, from elegant table wares to kitchen pots and an amazing variety of pottery and porcelain figures.

It is these figures which in recent years have captured the imagination of collectors more than the great flood of patterned services and general table ware, the more elaborate examples of which were once so sought after to decorate the corner cabinets of our parents and grandparents.

I have tried in this chapter to be practical when I have mentioned the names of potters who sometimes used a factory mark on their figures. You will indeed find others in the reference books and encyclopaedias but for the most part there is little point in discussing them in detail here since they hardly ever appear on the market. Having said that I shall immediately appear to contradict myself and write something about a family of Staffordshire potters called Tittensor of whose work in the first quarter of the nineteenth century I have only been able to trace records of but eleven marked examples. Such pieces impressed at the back of the figure TITTENSOR in capital letters within a sunken irregular oblong are, therefore, even more rare than the celebrated salt-glazed Pew Groups of the 1740s and are not easily found even in the great collections of the world famous museums.

So why do I bother to tell you all about them here? Well, even though these marked examples are so very rare and desirable it seems to me that collectors ought to be able to have a chance of seeing what they look like. They are very distinctive in several specific features and sometimes – not often but sometimes – unmarked examples have surfaced and been sold unrecognized for what they were. Almost certainly they will again and

35 & 36. Two highly important and extremely rare early groups both impressed Tittensor. *c.*1790. 7¾, 8 ins.

for a knowledgeable collector what greater thrill could there be than to find one covered with dust and tucked away in the corner of a village junk shop?

The name Tittensor appears in the parish records of the Potteries from the earliest days, but apart from a plaque signed by a Jacob Tittensor in 1789 the family seems to have worked mainly in the early part of the nineteenth century. Several Tittensors seem to have had connections with potting but the clearest documents refer to a Charles Tittensor working actively in Hanley and later in Shelton from about 1802–25.

It was, I believe, most likely Charles who made the two marked groups illustrated in Figures 35 and 36. At first sight they look very like some of the early Walton groups both in style and subject: rustic figures seated on a mound base dotted with sheep and surmounted by a leafy bocage. The similarity is superficial for upon closer inspection they differ in almost every particular. The figures are modelled by hand, not moulded. The green of the base is translucent like that of the Woods, and the cobalt blue on the figures and flowers is under the glaze, not enamelled over it, like the Walton pieces. The total range of the colours is limited and cool; yellow, pale orangey brown, blue and green, giving the whole a most attractive appearance. The little patches of colour on the cheeks are reminiscent of a much earlier period and indeed the *naïveté* of design and

37 & 38. The TITTENSOR mark impressed in a sunken irregular oblong.

decoration owes more to the eighteenth century than to the school of Walton in the nineteenth.

The veins of the bocage are incised not moulded, although in some photographs I have seen of similar marked specimens the bocage leaves do appear to be moulded, suggesting a slightly later date. But most interesting and characteristic of these early Tittensor groups is a series of incised diagonal and parallel lines on the side or the front of the base. (38) It is a feature that I have never found on the base of any other potter and where it occurs I would be prepared to accept the figure as genuine early Tittensor.

I say early because, as we have seen, the earliest records we have of Charles Tittensor would suggest that he was first potting about 1802. Now some authorities have dated these groups as late as 1820. Well some of them might be, there are some marked groups of Dandies with moulded bocage where the costumes of the figures are certainly Regency. However, these groups are much earlier than 1820. The costumes are late eighteenth century, and it would seem safer to say that Tittensor was probably working earlier than 1802, from the last years of the eighteenth century and continuing through the first quarter of the nineteenth.

This group of the boy and girl in Figure 35 is particularly interesting as it would appear that they may also have been made as a separate pair. TITTENSOR is impressed on the back of each of them. (37) They share a joined bocage with incised leaves and their individual bases each have a moulded decoration of a five petal flower enclosed by two fern leaves. Beneath this on the boy's figure is the impressed title SHEPERD. The girl's title is not so clear but the final S can be seen. Both figures are mounted and blended into the mound base which is incised with crude leaf designs and dotted with a hand modelled sheep and lambs.

Ralph Salt (1782–1846) later copied the figures as a separate pair with almost identical individual bases including the leaf fern and flower motif and the impressed titles SHEPERD and SHEPERDISS. They carried his impressed mark SALT at the back. In Salt's versions everything is made from moulds and decorated with bright enamel overglaze colours in the style of Walton.

This group is therefore a most important ceramic link. Charles Tittensor was christened in January 1764 and given his family connections it seems unlikely that he started potting at the late age of thirty-eight in 1802, the first recorded date we have for him as a working potter. I have not been able to find any evidence that he and Salt ever worked together, although it is possible. On stylistic grounds I would certainly date both these groups to the end of the eighteenth century, about 1790, and pre-dating the work of both Salt and Walton.

39. A different style of Tittensor potting, marked specimens have been recorded. c.1800. 5 ins.

The question is further complicated because there exists another quite different group of figures some of which bear the Tittensor mark. They are so completely different in style that one is tempted to wonder if they are perhaps potted by another member of the family. They usually depict two rather chubby cherubs supporting a central plaque or an urn. They are much more like the Neo-Classical school of Neale than the rustic school of Walton. (39)

They are usually said to be earlier than the first group but are much more likely to be contemporary. They are sophisticated in style, the cherubs carefully moulded and decorated in fine quality overglaze enamel colours. The simple stepped and rectangular bases are sometimes moulded with classical acanthus leaves or painted to imitate marble. Unmarked examples turn up quite often and since they are usually unattributed they are underpriced and more easily acquired by collectors.

Charles Tittensor is also known to have made transfer printed wares but it is his figures which appeal most. A potter of importance with great individuality and charm.

In case it may be thought strange that I do not include the name of Josiah Wedgwood as a maker of marked figures I must plead prejudice. He did certainly make some figures but they are cold and impersonal, more like little marble statues than pottery figures. I don't care for his other things either, however much they have been admired in the past. I find the man to be more like a confectioner than a potter, an icer of wedding cakes more than a moulder of native clay. There are some figures impressed with his name with some life and humanity in them but it now seems probable that they were made for him by other potters to supply a demand for a style he did not produce himself. Better let us consider his contemporaries and his successors more in touch with their own world. Most of them are unknown but their figures will speak for them.

3
Obadiah Sherratt
The Master of Burslem

With the end of the long war against France in 1815, the Potteries in Staffordshire produced and expanded with an enthusiasm encouraged by profits for the managers and the promise of a Methodist reward in heaven for the workers.

That sentence gives a picture as incomplete and facile as the empty outlines of the drawings in a child's colouring book. It is only as accurate as far as it goes. The workers had other spurs and comforts. The more able and adventurous of them set up on their own, instant managers overnight, their factories no more than a ramshackle hovel. Some of them were only part-time potters with other jobs on the side, ale-house keepers or grocers, while yet others scraped along as small family units using their children as unpaid labourers on a diet of crude porridge and beer.

It is this largely anonymous group of potters that produced many of the enchanting figures we love and collect today but it is true to say that we know more about the folk-art of ancient Egypt than we do of our own in the last century. There are records but they are sparse and often unreliable. By far the best research was published twenty-five years ago by Haggar, whose diligence in recording old parish records and contemporary newspaper accounts laid a foundation upon which all later serious research has been built. It was Haggar who lifted the curtain for me and confirmed my belief that there were two worlds in Staffordshire. Firstly, the world of the grand potters mostly established in the eighteenth century; commercial concerns of great standing like Minton, Davenport, the Ridgway family and Copeland and Garrett who succeeded Spode, to name only a few. Minton alone in 1858 was employing 1500 workers and all these factories were producing porcelain of fine quality designed for the tables of the rich. Minton did, it is true, produce some figures but they were of an elegance and sophistication more closely allied to the eighteenth century in style than to the new world of the Industrial Revolution.

Running parallel with these grand concerns was the fascinating sub-culture of the back-street potters and such records as we have of them are pitifully inadequate, no factory lists of artists and gilders, no beautifully drawn design books and more often than not no record of the very name of the potter himself. Modern bureaucracy with its endless documentation has a lot to answer for but it will at least smooth the path for future research into our own age. The division of cultures was not as sharp as a clean cut line. There were many potters of whom one could say that they were intermediate

40. Sherratt. *c.*1830. 7½ ins.

between the two groups, some of them successfully working their way up and some sinking into the poorest category through financial failure. But of these we often know little more than their names and occasionally the address where they worked. So without records we are left only with the things they made. Most of their output seems to have been of figures, variously referred to as images, toys or chimney ornaments. We should not complain, they are after all still with us in great numbers in spite of the unregarded thousands which have been broken, lost, or simply thrown away in times when the acme of ceramic taste was a simpering shepherdess with lace knickers. Some idea of the output of these tiny potteries may be judged from some facts I found in the State Paper Room of the British Library. In 1843 a little boy of nine, Robert Moreton, who worked for his father gave evidence to a Royal Commission on the Employment of Children in Industry.

> "I work by the piece and can make forty dozen small figures a
> day. I get a penny for ten dozen, that is two shillings [10p] a week.
> I work from seven to seven, sometimes eight or nine."

35

Well at least the poor little devil was paid, but just imagine the number of figures which must have poured out from those mucky little hovels during the nineteenth century. It is not surprising that their quality could vary enormously, some of them are so crude and misshapen that they have little value today except that of curiosity, and a sad curiosity at that. It doesn't do to let one's imagination run too free. Sometimes I see such a figure with its malformed face and twisted limbs and can imagine too clearly the little boy or girl who made it.

What is more truly amazing is that so many of them were of such fine quality. It has never been sufficiently acknowledged that some of the figures which cannot be attributed to any of the well known Staffordshire factories deserve to be judged by a very high standard, and that the finest of them, especially those made in a porcellaneous body, have been seriously underrated by all but a minority of both experts and collectors.

In my first book I described in some detail the actual process of manufacture but for our purpose now, it's enough to say that by the beginning of the nineteenth century most of the methods in use were past the experimental stage and no longer the jealously guarded secrets of their inventors. They were open to anyone with enough capital or credit to avail themselves of the bare minimum of basic materials, labour and a coal-fired bottle kiln which in some cases it seems likely may have been shared with other potters with limited funds. Experimentation with the actual body of the clay itself, however, did continue and produced some fascinating variations from crude opaque earthenware to surprisingly fine translucent porcelains with a range of bodies in between.

I understand a natural reluctance by some writers to avoid the subject of Staffordshire figures. Experts like facts: marks, design books, factory records, broken scraps of pottery, the shards and wasters found when excavating old factory sites so that attributions may be made with confidence. It makes things neat and tidy. But Staffordshire wasn't neat and tidy. It was a huge manufacturing area of heterogeneous potters merging and blending one into another, copying each other's commercial successes, luring good workers away from rivals – decorators, mould makers and modellers alike – and sometimes borrowing from each other not only ideas but the very clay with which they worked. No wonder some ceramic experts fight shy of it. If Winston Churchill had been discussing the Potteries and not Russia he couldn't have put it better, "It is a riddle wrapped in a mystery inside an enigma".

Later, when we come to examine the figures of the Victorian period, we shall see that they themselves can provide the best records, for they are more important than any set of names and addresses in that great huddle of mean streets and it is the figures which sometimes can reveal something of their origin and of the men who made them.

But before we come to the accession of Victoria, let's look at a contemporary of John Walton who potted in a very distinctive style making it possible to attribute figures to

41. Sherratt must have seen many travelling showmen like this. The bocage is Walton type but the bases confirm them as Sherratt. *c.*1820. 8½ ins.

him even though there was never a figure marked with his name.

Obadiah Sherratt was no less shadowy a person than Walton or any of the others. He was probably born about 1775 but nothing is known about his early life except a record of his marriage to an Ann Davenport in 1797. Haggar says that the church was in Norton-in-the-Moors and that this parish acquired a reputation for the marriages of non-resident parishioners, "a kind of Gretna Green for the Staffordshire Potteries", a fact which will be of interest when we look at some of his figures. When Ann died in 1810 Obadiah married again within two months, a widow named Martha Austin whose first marriage had also been registered at Norton-in-the-Moors.

In the trade directory for 1822–3 Obadiah is listed as a master potter, a toy and figure maker working in Hot Lane, Burslem. What else? Well, he moved to Waterloo Road about 1828 or 9 and he was still potting there in 1834. At some point between then and 1846 he either died or retired and the pot-bank was worked by his son Hamlet, and then in 1851 it was listed under the name of his wife Martha. And that virtually is that. Haggar found a record of an Obadiah Sherratt who kept an ale house in Longport Burslem in 1834 and from the only other evidence we have – that of his figures themselves – it seems likely that it was the same Obadiah.

The very distinctive style which has been traditionally ascribed to Obadiah Sherratt is usually easy to identify. He worked in a cruder, broader style than Walton and mounted his groups or figures on several different bases which have come to be accepted as by his hand. Sometimes he used a flat base, either decorated to look like marble or plain with one or two lines of coloured enamel. More frequently he favoured

42. Sherratt's wonderfully vulgar deities are based firmly on Burslem not Olympus.
*c.*1830. 10½ ins.

a base mounted upon four or six little legs about an inch high. There is a third type of Sherratt base less formal than either the plain flat slab or the table base. It is sometimes confused with a typical Walton style but can be distinguished by a motif or bright rainbow colours either in shallow loops or straight lines. (40)

Since I have mentioned inches you may see that throughout this book I have ignored centimetres. In my articles and advertisements I used to quote the heights of figures in both inches and centimetres and a great bore it was working it all out in those wretched decimals. However since no one ever took any notice of them and since the metric system obviously isn't going to catch on in England we might as well stick to what we all know and understand.

There is no documentary evidence that links Obadiah Sherratt with these groups and yet the attribution is firmly established by word of mouth and I accept it as being true. After all we are not going back all that far. What are we talking about? – a mere 150 odd years. It's not long ago, a few grandfathers away from us. It is a game we all play at some time or other, but I am still surprised when I reflect that the pink-faced old gentleman who presented me with a prize at school was a son of Queen Victoria and had been dandled on the knee of his godfather, the Duke of Wellington.

Sherratt then. Let us accept him with his earthy humour and his love of the travelling fairgrounds with their wonders emblazoned across the front of their wagons in colours as bright as those he used on the groups and figures he made to celebrate them. What I love about him is his obvious zest for life and for his own world about him. Poking fun at teetotallers but with enough commercial sense to pay lip service to

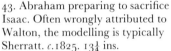

43. Abraham preparing to sacrifice Isaac. Often wrongly attributed to Walton, the modelling is typically Sherratt. c.1825. 13¼ ins.

44. This group suggests that Sherratt may have had a market in Northern Ireland or perhaps Liverpool for the symbols appear to be those of the Orange Order. c.1835. 10¼ ins.

the religious minded among his customers, although he made sure that they received the full blast of the Old Testament as well as the most sensational drama of the New. Not too proud to copy a Derby Neptune and Venus, he improves them immeasurably by giving us a Neptune from a fish-market instead of Olympus, and by similarly bringing Venus down to earth with a fashionable 1830s hairstyle.

Sherratt loved blood and thunder, he must have read – or been told (for there is some doubt about his literacy, he signed his marriage register with a cross) – of the fate which befell Lieutenant Hector Monroe in India on December 2nd 1792. This officer was engaged on that day not in any great campaign of arms, indeed nothing more warlike than a pleasant picnic with a few friends. "Having occasion," as one account puts it, "to retire into the surrounding undergrowth for a necessary moment, he was pounced on by a tiger while his attention and his natural caution were diverted." Another version of the drama which has the Lieutenant shooting deer when he was attacked was published in 1807, and it may well have been this which came to Sherratt's attention.

The horrid story, replete with gory details, made a deep impression upon the public at the time and Obadiah Sherratt's explicit version, Figure 45, would surely have satisfied the most bloodthirsty of his customers – the same customers who would have bought his vivid bull-baiting groups. There is without doubt an element of prurience in Sherratt, or perhaps he was simply a good businessman and gave others what they wanted. If they wanted murder and mayhem, whether it was a souvenir of the murder in the Red Barn with William Corder and his victim Maria Marten posed demurely

45. The Death of Lieutenant Hector Monroe in India, 1792. Sherratt. *c*.1815. 10½ ins.

46. Titled view of the Red Barn at Polestead. Sherratt. *c*.1828. 6 ins.

40

47. William Corder and his victim Maria Marten. 48. Dr Syntax. Ralph Salt. *c*.1820. 5½ ins.
He buried her in the Red Barn at Polestead and
was executed in 1828. Sherratt. *c*.1828. 8 ins.

side by side on a table base, or the infamous Red Barn itself, Sherratt was your man.
(46, 47)

Perhaps if you lived and worked in Burslem in that early nineteenth century it was easy to become cruel and coarsened. In 1829, the year after the Red Barn murder, Simeon Shaw wrote a history of the Staffordshire Potteries. It is an invaluable book for research workers, with a contemporary account of the techniques of manufacture, the composition of clays and descriptions of how the figures were decorated. Shaw describes Burslem as "a flourishing place with many wide and spacious new streets of excellent dwelling houses". The key word here is "new". Shaw had enough sense to know that his book, which he had privately printed by a local bookseller, would do well in the Potteries if he said nice things about it and the people who worked there. As an exercise in sycophancy this book is a model. Never were so many saints and paragons of virtue and benevolence gathered together to shower blessings upon their grateful and contented workers. Two worlds again. If we look at an account of the same town in the 1840s as remembered by an old man who had worked there as a child, we find it a very different Burslem. The wide spacious streets are not what he remembers but mean,

41

narrow alleys running with open sewers and lined with tumbledown cottages little better than pig sties. The Burslem of that little boy was known as "the hell hole" where children worked twelve to fourteen hours a day and were thrashed with a rope stiffened with hardened clay if they fell asleep as they made pottery figures of "the gentlest of swains and the sweetest of maids".

That world was nearer to Sherratt than the one Simeon Shaw chose to present.

Everything in Sherratt's figures is a little crude and garish, for he reflected the age he lived in. The bocage is broader in design and the pattern of decoration on his women's skirts bigger and less finely painted than Walton's. Yet the overall effect is hugely successful like a brass band in the sun or a fanfare of trumpets at Polito's Travelling Menagerie. Some of Sherratt's groups are much rarer than others. It isn't likely that you will find his Polito's Menagerie easily nowadays and if you did it would be worth a lot of money. I didn't say expensive, but a lot of money and certainly worth it – a better buy, more sound and sure, than any stocks or shares could ever be. It is Sherratt's masterpiece and can be accurately dated to about 1808, for Polito died in April 1814 and his wife in July. The menagerie visited Wolverhampton in 1808 about thirty miles away from Sherratt in Burslem and he must surely have either seen it for himself or a circus poster with a drawing from which he worked. No, he must have seen it for himself; it is so alive and so full of colour. It is as English as Hogarth and Dickens and nothing which came out of the Staffordshire Potteries in those years before Victoria so exactly captures the magic and wonder of the travelling fairground. Sherratt's shaky spelling does nothing to diminish the charm of the title impressed boldly across Polito's parade wagon, "Polito's Menagerie of the Wonderful Burds and Beasts from Most Parts of the World, Lions, etc". It is more than a title, it is as inviting and irresistible as the trumpets and drum and the dancing monkey on the hurdy-gurdy guarding the door closed upon the marvels within. (Colour Plate I)

Within a few years the fairgrounds were to make a tremendous impression upon the potters during Victoria's reign, but it was Sherratt who captured it first and no one ever did it better. Not all his figures are as rare as this, many of them do still appear on the market and no collection of pre-Victorian figures should be without at least one. Some of them sell today at prices lower than some Victorian pieces.

In a way Sherratt was ahead of his time. His palette of colours, his use of bocage, is influenced by the style of his contemporaries. Where he differs from them is the way he adapts them and in his choice of subjects.

There is a close affinity in his work to the caricature cartoonists. Although Hogarth and Gillray were essentially eighteenth century, their work had little or no influence on the Staffordshire potters apart from a few scurrilous transfer prints on jugs and mugs during the Napoleonic war. Sherratt may well have seen their work and that of Rowlandson and the young George Cruikshank, whose series of drawings on the evils of drink are paralleled in Sherratt's two groups titled "Ale Bench" and "Tee Total".

49 & 50. Sherratt
made five or six
different versions of
Bull-baiting groups
with various bases and
titles. *c.*1830. 9,
9½ ins.

51. Ralph Wood lions look like pet pussycats compared with Sherratt's vigorous "Roring Lion". *c.*1830. 9 ins.

(Colour Plate II) Ralph Salt, whose dates approximate very closely to Sherratt's, had certainly seen Rowlandson's drawings of the three tours of Dr Syntax (48) for he stamped his mark on figures of the caricatured Doctor, but it was Sherratt who reflected the humour and satire of his day to a far greater degree. Like Walton he was a bridge between the eighteenth and nineteenth centuries but he looked forward to themes and subjects that were to be more fully explored by his successors in the Victorian era. He did, in fact, go on potting into that period but his work could never be confused with the Victorians.

The analogy with the cartoonist is important because it points towards a new movement in the style of the Staffordshire potters. Apart from the very small number of little, hand-moulded toy figures like the salt-glazed Pew Groups in the 1740s, the Potteries in the eighteenth century largely ignored contemporary themes. The figures and groups they made were influenced by, and catered almost exclusively for, a cultured minority. Not entirely for the aristocracy but for an educated and monied class who could afford to eat from fine decorated plates, to drink expensive tea from delicate cups and saucers and to admire a few exquisitely contrived pottery and

44

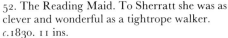

52. The Reading Maid. To Sherratt she was as clever and wonderful as a tightrope walker. *c.*1830. 11 ins.

53. The Engagement. Sometimes on a table base and titled "Perswaition". No wonder Sherratt admired little girls who could read and spell. *c.*1820. 8 ins.

porcelain figures in a china cabinet. These figures were influenced by the factories of Chelsea and of Derby and Bow which in turn had drawn their inspiration from Germany and China to delight an Age of Reason and an Age of Elegance.

It was Sherratt who pointed out that there was more to a bull than the seductive gentle porcelain creature who enticed the beautiful Europa on to his back to swim away with her for love and dalliance on the island of Crete. Sherratt's bulls were bold and bloody, goaded and tormented by dogs especially bred for the appalling ritual and encouraged to do so by men who thought it sport. Both the dogs and the poor tethered bull suffered cruelties which I cannot bring myself to describe. Sherratt knew, because without any question he had seen the horror for himself and recorded it in clay. (49, 50)

These bull-baiting groups on both flat and table bases are still much sought after by collectors but do beware of a small one about $5\frac{1}{4}$ inches high and $7\frac{1}{2}$ inches wide. It is nicely potted although the glaze and the colours are wrong for Sherratt. It was produced by the William Kent factory and was last quoted in their catalogue for 1960. Some years ago when I was doing some research in the Potteries, I spoke to the man who had reduced it in size and potted it for the Kent factory. He had one of them in a

54. Marriage at Gretna Green. Sherratt has moulded a horse on his table base, presumably the
runaways' transport to the forge. c.1820. 8¼ ins.

55. The Christening. Sherratt. c.1825. 8½ ins.

56. Knowing Obadiah Sherratt's predilection for the more notorious forms of vulgar entertainment, it may seem odd that he should have chosen to make this bust of the beautiful young actress Maria Foot (1797–1867). Odd, that is, until you know that she was not only a famous star of Covent Garden and Drury Lane but that her private life was scandalous and fiercely debated for many years in newspapers and pamphlets. She was not afraid to face her critics and indeed was as well known in the provinces as Polito's Menagerie, travelling more than 2,500 miles by stage coach to theatres all over the Kingdom. She had many lovers, two illegitimate children and won a breach of promise action for the then enormous sum of £3,000. She was highly talented both on and off the stage where she was equally at home as a dramatic actress and a singer. One of her most successful songs was "Where are you going to my pretty maid?" A question she answered convincingly in 1831 when she retired from the stage on 11th March and on 7th April married Charles Stanhope, 4th Earl of Harrington. c.1816. 12 ins.

57. *The Grecian and Daughter* or *Roman Charity*, was originally a late eighteenth century play based on the legend of Cimon and Pera. An abridged version was a great favourite in the travelling theatres. Cimon is starving in prison and only saved by being breast-fed by his daughter Pera. A melodramatic aspect of family life which obviously fascinated Sherratt. *c*.1830. 9 ins.

58. Not a typical base for Sherratt although the bocage and figures are unmistakably his and, of course, the New Marriage Act was very much his sort of subject. Passed in 1836 it permitted legal marriage in churches and chapels outside the Church of England, but henceforth all of them, the established church included, had to supply the civil registrar with an exact copy of the entry recorded in the vestry. Sherratt seems to have regarded this as unnecessary pedantry, the plaque reads: The New Marriage Act. John Frill and Ann Boke, Aged 21. That is right says the Parson. Amen says the clerk. *c*.1836. 7 ins.

little cabinet in his living room and was very proud of it in his retirement. It bears a very good copy of a Sherratt-type title in lozenge-shaped cartouches. At a sale in the Midlands in October 1980, one of these modern reproductions incorrectly catalogued as Obadiah Sherratt aroused great interest in a crowded sale-room and was bought for £374 including the sale-room premium. The original titled Sherratt group is about 12 inches high and like many of his figures the glaze tends to be rather dry looking.

So there he is, Obadiah Sherratt of Hot Lane, Burslem – master potter, maker of wonderful figures and groups where bulls roared and wives screeched at drunken husbands, where the awful piety of Abraham was forever about to plunge a dagger in his little son's throat and Christ prayed in Agony while man-eating tigers carried off poor army Lieutenants for a horrid picnic.

His work has been known and collected for years but I believe his importance has been much underestimated. He has been popular but not appreciated for the revolutionary nature of his work. Sherratt was the first potter to comment on his social scene to a significant degree. The Woods were finer technicians but they only made two

60. Sherratt's Flight into Egypt. *c.*1830. 9 ins.
59. The marriage theme again. Sherratt's version of The Judgement of Paris. The story had been popular since Congreve's masque in 1701. Many early nineteenth century versions were performed in the travelling fairground theatres. Paris holds the apple in his hand. Unrecorded. *c.*1830. 13½ ins.

tentative forays into humour with their "Parson and Clerk" and "The Vicar and Moses" both of which look pretty insipid compared with Sherratt's robust vulgarities.

What he saw around him was poverty, cruelty and drunkenness. Of what use were the Roman gods and legends to Sherratt's world? Jupiter and Minerva were for the shelves of the landed gentry and the new manufacturing rich who aped them. For the poor and the hungry there was a grimmer world with new gods. The god of Wesley fighting the temptations of the bottle in ale houses like The Foaming Quart where a man would drink his money away from Saturday to Monday or Tuesday, content to make up his work quota in a four-day marathon until Saturday came again.

Sherratt looked at Olympus and saw that it was meaningless. He looked at the classical lions of the Woods and gave us his "Roring Lion" of the menageries. He couldn't spell it but he had seen it. His "Reading Maid" is not a gentle portrait of a good little girl but a shout of triumph and wonder that a child could read at all. He made it because he saw the beginnings of education in the kitchens of old women who taught a lucky few of the ragged children for pennies until they started to work at the mature age of six or seven, and he saw the new Sunday Schools in Wesley's chapels where the children paid nothing at all. (52)

It was a new world. The eighteenth century was over and Sherratt saw it and brought it down to earth. Perhaps there was a gentler side to his nature: when he made a group of young lovers with the boy offering the maid an engagement ring; and when he showed perhaps the same youngsters being married before the blacksmith's anvil at Gretna Green, might Sherratt not have remembered his own marriage at Norton-in-the-Moors, the Gretna Green of the potteries? (53, 54, 55)

4
Animals

Animals in Staffordshire Pottery are much sought after, but curiously little has been written about them for collectors to consult.

In the eighteenth century the Woods made some charming animal figures. Most of them were of the domestic variety: dogs, goats, squirrels, sheep, pigs, foxes and deer. I put these into the domestic category to separate them from the rather more exotic beasts which they also produced like lions, monkeys and even a very poor attempt at an elephant. All the Wood animals tend to be a bit influenced by the classical school and often sit rather stiffly on plinth bases with a formal motif of moulded leaves. Not all of them, however; some of their small animals sit more suitably on grassy mounds giving them a more natural look. Probably the most attractive animal figure they ever made was a delightful pet squirrel wearing a collar and chewing a nut. It dates from about 1775 and is entirely English in conception. But you can't get the Woods away from Olympus easily and they couldn't resist dotting their lions and lionesses with revolting

61. Stag and Fox. Ralph Wood, coloured glaze. *c.*1780. 5 ins.

62. Pet Squirrel with collar. Ralph Wood, coloured glaze. *c.*1775. 7¼ ins.

50

63. Hind and Stag. Ralph Wood,
coloured glaze. *c.*1775. $4\frac{7}{8}$, $6\frac{3}{4}$ ins.

64. Lioness with *putti*. Ralph Wood, coloured
glaze. *c.*1770. $8\frac{1}{2}$ ins.

65. Sheep. Ralph Wood,
coloured glaze. c.1785. 3½ ins.

66. Ram. Ralph Wood, coloured glaze. c.1785. 4¼ ins.

little winged cupids. They did a bull-baiting group (7) but it's a poor thing compared with the terrifying reality with which Sherratt treated the subject. (49, 50) Even so, a collection of animals should certainly aim to have at least one example of their work. (61–66)

It's odd that cats are very rare in any period. Perhaps there are more dogs because of their close connection with sport and cats are far too sensible to hunt for anyone but themselves. There are some lovely little agate striped cats which were made about 1750 but they are rare enough to command a high price when they come on to the market. There are some examples in museums like Hanley and the Fitzwilliam, worth a visit for a collector to see and to admire them but hardly a practical proposition for people of average means. (67)

67. Agate-ware cat. c.1745. 4¾ ins.

Polito's Menagerie. Obadiah Sherratt *c.*1808. 11½ ins.

Camden P. 6

68. A collection of Staffordshire pottery and porcelain cats. Late eighteenth, early nineteenth centuries. Tallest 2½ ins.

There is a Neale figure of a little girl in a mob-cap, lovingly clasping a pet cat in her arms, which would grace any animal collection, girl or no girl. And very occasionally a stray cat turns up in Pratt-ware or with sponged enamel colours dabbed on to suggest the odd marking to which stray cats are prone. It is not always easy to date them accurately. Some are obviously late eighteenth century, crude little toys probably made for children. Cats made from a red clay and covered by a very fine underglaze black, lightly decorated with gold, are generally supposed to have been made by a potter called Maurice Thursfield at the Jackfield pottery in Shropshire, but many workmen from that factory came to Staffordshire where they produced similar examples. Later on, the Victorians made some gloriously smug pussycats sitting demurely on bases of deep cobalt blue.

It was to be the Victorians who produced more animal figures in Staffordshire than at any other period in its long history and it came about because of the travelling menageries and fairgrounds.

There had always been a tradition of fairground entertainment in England but it was the Victorians who developed and promoted them beyond anything that had gone before. What wonderful places were those fairs! To understand what a tremendous influence they had on the production of animal figures by the potters we should look more closely at them, for their history is largely the history of the pottery animal figures in Victorian England and there are still enough of those to make them easily available to collectors. The fairs not only influenced the production of animal figures, they were a

69. The original model by Thomas Parr. *c.*1849. 7½ ins. Much reproduced. A modern version is listed in the Kent catalogue (107). 7 ins.

key factor in the growing popularity of melodrama. If we can examine the fairgrounds of the nineteenth century we shall be able to understand much more about the figures produced, both the animals and the exotic performers who travelled with them all over the British Isles.

Even as I begin to tell the story I get a feeling of fun and excitement, and really that is what true collecting is all about, or should be. No one should collect purely as a hedge against inflation. If your collection increases in value then that is an added bonus but it degrades the art of collecting if that is to be the sole aim. No collection can be ours for ever; we add to it and learn more about it as the years go by. Piece by piece it grows, each one making the whole greater than its parts and we are only caretakers for others who will come after us, that is our privilege. Collections which are built up like a whirlwind with the cheque book as the sole arbiter and then dumped on the market for a profit are not really collections at all but goods and chattels abandoned for gain. That is the wrong kind of fun and excitement. To be a collector you need more than money, you need love and a sense of adventure and fun.

Fun and excitement were the sole aims of the fairs. For at least two hundred years before the Norman Conquest groups of "itinerant professors in the art of amusing, dancers, posturers, jugglers, tumblers and exhibitors of trained monkeys and quadrupeds" tramped from town to town and village to village in search of fresh audiences. Gentle unmechanized nomads supplying a need for villagers and nobles alike. Their performances altered very little through the centuries until the population explosion and the Industrial Revolution changed everything.

In 1818 a lady lay on her back on the ground in a tent in the middle of a field in Croydon. On her stomach was a blacksmith's anvil weighing 400 lbs. upon which a gentleman was busy forging horseshoes with a heavy hammer. Earlier she had lifted a table five feet long and three feet wide with two people and a begging dog seated upon it, a considerable feat in itself but more so since she had lifted it with her teeth. She had further obliged her goggle-eyed audience, who had paid a penny each to see her, by lifting the anvil by her hair and swinging it to and fro between her legs.

Madame Gobert, The French Female Hercules, was not the sole attraction in that Croydon field. There was a horse with seven legs (six of them shod), a singing pig accompanied on the flute by her owner and trainer Signor Fortunati and "The Little Wonder". This last, billed as "The Learned Horse", could count, spell, tell the time, return handkerchiefs to their rightful owners and select ladies among the crowd who, "were longing to get married but were too shy to say so". Tiring from such mental exertion he sat tidily up at a nursery table and shared his supper with a clown, leaving a bevy of bright-eyed girls, red shiny-faced with embarrassed ardour to explain themselves in detail to the farm boys who had brought them to the fair and might live to regret it forever. (70)

When the great Trade Fairs began to become firmly established at fixed dates and places attracting customers from great distances and lasting sometimes as long as sixteen days, they were a natural target for every horse who could count up to ten and every lady capable of supporting a blacksmith's anvil on her stomach.

The showmen had found a large captive audience and in our period they were to become a greater attraction than the traders themselves. The Victorians exploited commercially the scientific discoveries of the previous century. Country people left the cottage industries of the villages, and the new towns, ill equipped to minister to their health or their entertainment, received them in their hundreds of thousands.

This was the ultimate audience for the showmen of the fairs. They saw that the cramped masses in the towns were as hungry for fun and glamour as they were for food. They need no longer rely solely upon the limited numbers and static locations of the Trade Fairs, the new towns were waiting for them and the travelling fairs exploited the new possibilities to the full, expanding as the demand for new wonders increased.

In earlier years a few wild animals had been exhibited usually as single attractions. For the young Victorians this was not enough and the new fairs supported whole menageries of exotic creatures from the ends of the earth. The names of the menageries travelling with the fairs like Polito, Wombwell, Ballard, Atkins, Manders and Sangers were known everywhere. Giraffes, camels, lions, tigers, elephants, leopards, zebras, monkeys, boa constrictors and an odoriferous host of other beasts were confined in cages and hauled laboriously by cart horses from one centre to another to be gawped at by wide-eyed workers who inspected them at closer quarters than most African villagers had ever done or ever wanted to. (71–83) In 1911 "Lord" George Sanger in

70. The Learned Horse. Based on a print of the clown John
Ducrow. The act was a favourite all over the country and it is
odd that so far this is the only known Staffordshire figure of it to
survive. *c.*1845. 7 ins.

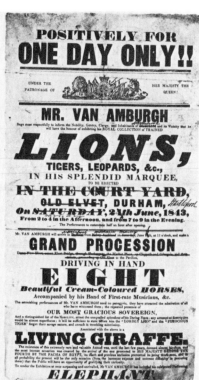

71. Menagerie and Van Amburgh posters, 1865 and 1843. Reproduced from *Victorian Delights* by courtesy of Evans Brothers Ltd.

72. Baby giraffes with travelling circus or menagerie keepers. *c*.1848. 9½, 9¾ ins.

73. *c*.1848. 7¼ins.

74. The giraffe in the centre is original, *c*.1848. The smaller pair with palm trees are modern Kent figures. *c*.1960. 5½, 7¼, 5½ ins.

75. These travelling menagerie camels are original but like all Staffordshire animals there are many late reproductions. *c*.1854. 5 ins.

76. The highlight of Van Amburgh's circus performance was to make a fierce lion lie down with a lamb. There would always have been a ready market for this pair. *c*.1848. 10 ins.

77. The Anglo-French war scare of 1860 changed Napoleon III from an ally into a potential enemy. Some paler modern reproductions turn up but the moulds are poor compared with these originals. *c*.1860. 9 ins.

78. Fine quality pair of travelling menagerie leopards. *c*.1845. 5¼ ins.

79. Leopard spill vases. Matches were expensive in the nineteenth century so children rolled strips of paper into spills to light at the fire. *c*1850. 6¾ ins.

80. Circus elephant spill vases. *c*.1850. 5¾ ins.

II Tee Total and Ale Bench. Obadiah Sherratt *c*.1830. 8¼ ins.

81. When zebras first appeared in the menageries the potters used these moulds of horses and painted them to look like zebras (note the flowing manes). *c.*1845. 8 ins.

82. Correctly moulded zebras with short manes. *c.*1858. 6 ins. Many later reproductions exist.

83. Many fairground theatres produced plays with monkey heroes. Actors disguised in masks and skins played the parts and were very popular. *c.*1834. 5¼ ins.

84. This poster is dated 1875 but the show had remained virtually unchanged since the 1840s. Reproduced from *Victorian Delights* by courtesy of Evans Brothers Ltd.

his book *Seventy Years a Showman* said that there was not a town or village of over one hundred inhabitants he had not visited. It is difficult for us to realize the enormous impression such exotic animals must have made on the minds of simple country people, or even on the inhabitants of large towns. The lady in *Punch* who beheld a giraffe for the first time and announced flatly that she didn't believe it, was not alone in her amazement. Today animals from the remotest corners of the world charge across our living rooms in full television colour leaving no stern untoned, they have become as familiar to us as the unconcerned cat on the hearthrug but then, of course, no wild animal escapes from a television set.

In Victorian days there were dramas in plenty. When the animals weren't attacking and mauling their keepers, their frequent escapes into short-lived freedom made startling newspaper stories and ensured even better business in the next town. "Oh Sir!" gasped an incredulous servant girl reporting an elephant in the kitchen garden to her master, "There's a girt big beast outside, 'tis pulling up cabbages with its tail and where 'tis putting them I daresn't tell you!"

And there were more wonders to come: circuses, waxwork exhibitions and the theatre itself. Scowton's Travelling Theatre and Richardson's (where the great Edmund Kean began his career) were quick to jump aboard the rolling bandwaggon with the menageries, circuses and sideshows. They added their names to the fairground scene glittering in rainbow-coloured gothic letters lit by the flares of naphtha oil. The gentle swings and sedate roundabouts of earlier days gained muscles and voices of steam as the mechanical organs blared out in happy cacophonous competition with the brass bands of Richardson's Theatre, Polito's Menagerie and Rowland's Colossal Exhibition of five hundred life-sized waxwork figures animated by clockwork.

It was now all of a piece, and this leviathan of combined delights, The Victorian Fair in all its glory, rolled cumbrously through the lanes and highways, blocking bridges in Scotland and defying the hills and torrents of Wales, bringing colour and magic to the town slaves and the even poorer farm workers who had never seen anything more exciting than elderly village Morris Dancers whose knee joints cracked louder than the elm sticks they decorously clacked together in self-conscious and be-ribboned rustic jollity.

Now it was the turn of the traders to use the crowds attracted by the entertainers. By 1820 the stalls in the fairgrounds were selling fruit, oysters, ale, gin, gingerbread, ribbons, household goods and toys. The latter at prices ranging from a halfpenny to ten shillings. As we know, the Staffordshire potters called their brightly coloured figures toys and the toy sellers had the largest stalls in the fair, some of them having a frontage of twenty-five feet.

The Industrial Revolution which had transformed the fairs had done the same for the potters of Staffordshire. With improved technical methods of production the potters filled the toy shops of the fairs with gaily coloured images of the young Queen Victoria and her family who rubbed shoulders on the shelves with heroes, statesmen, murderers, actors, circus performers and, of course, animals. Contrary to long established myth they were not given away as prizes, that fate was rightly reserved for the cheap little porcelain horrors known as fairings imported from Europe much later in the century. The Staffordshire figures were as English as the workers who made them and the people who bought them. They were sold elsewhere too, of course, in china shops, and hawked from village to hamlet by travelling "Cheap Johns", but the stalls of

85. Typical costumes for actors and dancers in the travelling theatres right through the nineteenth century. These figures are *c.*1848, *c.*1845, *c.*1849. 10¾, 12½, 11 ins.

the fairgrounds must have accounted for a large part of the trade and especially for the figures of animals. There can be little doubt that the many Victorian Staffordshire figures hitherto thought to be purely decorative were inspired by, and made specifically for, sale in the travelling fairs. The plumed head-dresses and curious ermined-edged costumes relating to no definite period of history are exactly the style favoured by the players in Richardson's travelling theatre and by the performers in circuses like Batty's, Cook's, Weldon's, Hengler's and Sanger's. (85, 86)

Almost always the potters' original source of information and inspiration was a print which they copied, simplified and adapted to produce their naïve and delightful pottery figures which have remained with us sometimes long after the original source has disappeared. In doing so they have left us many puzzles of identification to be solved. Sometimes luck and research combine to unearth a long forgotten print, the unquestionable original source for an untitled figure. If the print bears the name of its subject then we can identify the pottery portrait beyond any doubt. Few areas of antique research are so rewarding or satisfying.

Fairground posters were a rich source of inspiration for the potters. Staffordshire groups of zebras being attacked by pythons or mauled by lions are obvious examples, and it is sad that comparatively few of them have survived. When I recently examined

86. Two of the famous Lion Queens from Wombwell's Menagerie. Nellie Chapman on the left wisely retired unscathed in 1848 and was succeeded by Ellen Bright who was torn to pieces in 1850 at Chatham. *c.*1847, 1850. 11¾, 15 ins.

a Rowland's Waxworks poster I was interested to see that of the thirty-eight personalities or scenes advertised no less than twenty-five of them also appear in Staffordshire pottery. That poster was printed to publicize the fair's appearance in East Hartlepool for one day only, so it's a wonder it has survived at all, but it provides evidence of a hitherto unsuspected source from which the potters drew for many of their contemporary productions. (84)

A really big star like the American lion tamer Isaac Van Amburgh was famous enough to justify the potters issuing a titled portrait figure of him. (See Chapter 6.) He toured all over the country for years so that they were assured of steady sales. But there were dozens of lion tamers in the smaller fairs who imitated him, forcing open lions' jaws with scant courtesy, inserting their heads and bellowing down the poor beasts' throats.

Untitled Staffordshire figures depicting this act are not rare. They are frequently sold as portraits of Van Amburgh but common commercial sense suggests that they served equally well for any of the others. (87)

The lion tamers and wild beast shows were enormously popular and the myths and legends which were carefully cultivated about them ensured good business for the fairs and the potters alike. Everyone heard of the tragic death of Manchester Jack, Wombwell's lion tamer. From the depths of the lion's great mouth he anxiously enquired of his assistant, "Does he whisk his tail, Bill?" "Yes," said Bill. "Then I am a

66

87. "Does he whisk his tail, Bill?"
Lion Tamer. *c.*1860. 12½ ins.

dead man," groaned Manchester Jack and flash! Upon that instant the lion bit his head clean off.

Not true; not true at all. Manchester Jack retired unscathed and kept a pub in Taunton where he died in his bed in 1865. It was glamour, it was good business, and it was the stuff that dreams and Staffordshire figures were made of.

Contemporary accounts have preserved some faint shadow of what the Victorian fairgrounds were like. Where they have survived, the advertising posters which were plastered along the route ahead of the fair do even better. Their colour, typography and hyperbole bring the very smell of excitement and wonder into our sad, computerized century. Not many of them have survived. Their very nature and purpose, pasted as they were on walls and tree trunks, doomed them as ephemera. But the potters of Staffordshire saw them before the wind and the rain and the fingers of little boys sent the rainbow-coloured strips and tatters into the ditches and gutters for ever.

The potters saw and transformed them into the gaily coloured figures we know and love. They were to come safely down to us through the years, to brighten and cheer us and remind us of the days when pigs sang and horses could count, when heroines were saved from impossible villains by impossible heroes, when ferocious beasts of Africa roared defiance to the skies of England, and ladies danced on wires and rode naked on the backs of galloping wild stallions, and when a tired little dairymaid walked home

88. Rabbits with lettuce leaves. *c.*1850. 5½ ins.

89. Floppy eared rabbits. *c.*1860. 5¾ ins.

through the dark lanes with a farm boy who asked her to marry him and only just managed not to drop the Staffordshire figure he had bought her at the fair.

Not all the animal figures sold in the fairgrounds were exotic. There are some fine rabbits, foxes, dogs, birds and more rarely, cats. Staffordshire birds in the nineteenth century were wonderfully bizarre creatures. Decorated in every conceivable admixture of bright enamel colours they suggest the wildest fantasies of Walt Disney combined with the *naïveté* of Le Douanier Rousseau. They look like an ornithologist's

I A selection of early porcelain pastille burners 1820–1830, tallest 6½ ins.

90. Spill vases, foxes
with cubs. *c.*1852.
$7\frac{3}{4}$ ins.

91. Finely
modelled Labrador
Retriever pair.
*c.*1860. $7\frac{1}{4}$ ins.

92. Pointers by Thomas
Parr. *c.*1852. 5, 4 ins.

93. King Charles Spaniel marked Copeland and Garrett. *c.*1833. 2½ ins.

nightmare but they were not made for birdwatchers but to brighten up the dark mantel-shelves of humble cottages. (94)

Horses without an accompanying human figure can be found but they are quite rare. (95–98) The earliest zebras were simply made from the same mould as the horses complete with flowing manes, later ones have the correct brush mane. It's worth remarking here on the sheer cleverness and artistry of some of those unidentified figure makers. Just look and wonder at the leaping deer in Figure 99. It's hard to believe that such beauty of motion was achieved with a simple two-piece press mould, and yet the potter has captured the very moment of action like a modern high-speed camera.

Commonest of all, I suppose, are the familiar pairs of seated spaniel dogs, or Comforters as they were known. It's a good name because they are just that; quiet, soothing, delightfully smug, but certainly faithful and comforting. Curiously they are the most popular of all with my continental customers. The Danes, French, Germans, and Spanish all love them because they are so very English; perhaps for the very qualities listed above. I've only just thought of that but it's as good a reason as any. Their popularity has created a demand impossible to supply with the genuine antique

71

94. The fabled Roc bird carrying off a child. *The Arabian Nights* was first translated into English in 1840. This figure dates from *c.*1860. 13½ ins.

IV Isaac Van Amburgh. The American lion tamer as he appeared before Queen Victoria at
Drury Lane Theatre in 1838. John and Rebecca Lloyd of Shelton c.1838. 6¼ ins.

95. These riderless horses were inspired by the ring performances of the travelling circus and were sometimes decorated as zebras. *c.*1845. 8 ins.

96. Circus ponies with gold stars on the forehead. *c.*1855. 5½ ins.

74

97. A fine early Pratt-ware horse rearing over a man. *c.*1800. 8 ins.

98. The tradition of skilful modelling in Staffordshire survived throughout the nineteenth century. This horse was made by the Kent factory. *c.*1900. 11 ins.

99. Simplicity and economy of design in a two-piece mould by Sampson Smith of Longton. *c*.1870. 10½ ins.

dogs and there is a huge trade in modern reproductions faked to look old; more than any other Staffordshire pottery figures they are being made today in their thousands.

How can you tell? Well, it's not easy, some of them are very cleverly made expressly to fool even careful buyers. The fakers have, in fact, considerably improved upon their earlier efforts. One of my collectors suggested that I was largely to blame by writing articles describing the fakes in such detail that the forgers were learning from me what mistakes to avoid. I suppose there could be some truth in that, but there are such great numbers of modern reproductions floating around that I can at least give some idea of what to avoid.

The easiest to detect are those which have a pronounced close-meshed crackle stained with a brown dye to give a crude impression of age. The gilding, when it is attempted, has often been wiped to simulate wear and the glaze is poor with no depth or clarity; if you rub your thumb over it lightly it tends to drag unlike the feeling you get from a true lead glaze over which the thumb should slide as it would over the surface of a wine glass. Later efforts have abandoned the stained crackle but the glaze is still poor and like the earlier fakes the general quality of the decoration is much cruder than the originals. Look closely at the way the brown or black patches of colour have been

76

V Crimean War. *c.*1855. 13½ ins.

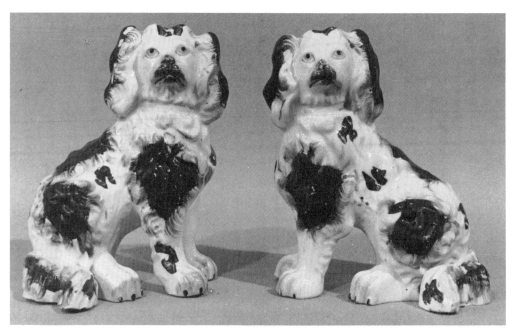

100. Comforter dogs were popular over a long period in the nineteenth century. Most of them date from 1860 onwards. This selection (100–103) shows some of the earlier examples. This fine pair is c.1845. 7 ins.

painted. Even though the originals were often painted by children working in appallingly bad conditions there is a delicacy and lightness of touch which the reproductions have never succeeded in copying. (100–104)

The difficulty is that one must distinguish between those modern reproductions which are made to look old with the express purpose of deceiving the buyer and those which were and indeed still are being made as honest reproductions for sale as such. The cricket magazine *Wisden* carried a full page advertisement on its back cover for the issue of November 1980. The advertisement offers for sale modern replicas of six rare Staffordshire figures and groups of cricketers together with a titled figure of W. G. Grace. This last is potted in the style of Victorian Staffordshire although in fact no titled original figure of W. G. Grace was ever made.

Now the advertisement makes it quite clear that all these figures are reproductions and indeed the prices quoted, which range from £17.50 to £39, underline the fact, for the originals are worth a great deal more than that. (105)

The difficulty, of course, arises when such figures have changed hands several times and are later dishonestly offered for sale as genuine originals at grossly inflated prices. Many of them have already found their way into country sale-rooms and antique markets to trap the unwary collector. Like the originals, they bear no factory mark and

101. Comforter dogs
with puppies. c.1840.
5 ins.

102. This
attractive and
unusual base
dates from
about 1853.
7¾ ins.

103. Cobalt
blue base.
c.1840. 6½ ins.

VI Sir Robert Peel. *c.*1850. 13 ins.

104. A more usual Comforter type by Sampson Smith on the left *c.*1860. The central money-box and the dog on the right are modern reproductions. *c.*1980. 7¼, 4, 6¾ ins.

105. Village cricket groups. *c.*1845. 6½ ins. Modern reproductions are now being made. *c.*1981. 6½ ins.

106–110. The Kent catalogue for 1960 by courtesy of Mr John S. Kent, who informs me that the figures are still being made in the Potteries under a different management.

as reproductions they are among the best I have seen. When they are first sold they look very new but some of those we have been shown seem to have aged dramatically since then.

William Kent (Porcelains) Ltd., of Burslem has an honourable history of figure production going back into the nineteenth century. They continued to make excellent reproductions of some of their nineteenth century figures up to the year 1962 when they abandoned their figure-making to concentrate on the manufacture of industrial porcelain. Unfortunately for collectors their figures were not marked and now that some of them have begun to acquire some age of their own they are often sold by dishonest or ignorant dealers as nineteenth century originals.

The Kent factory published a catalogue which in the 1960 edition listed over 370 figures, many of them animals. (106–110, 137) Cats sitting on cushions, Dalmatian dogs, deer, spaniels, sheep, cows, bulls, zebras, birds, camels, foxes, elephants, horses, lions, squirrels and, of course, whippets with or without rabbits, were just a fraction of their very comprehensive output.

Whippets were a great favourite with poor working people in Victorian days. They didn't eat much and they sometimes provided a free rabbit for the pot – a luxury for the

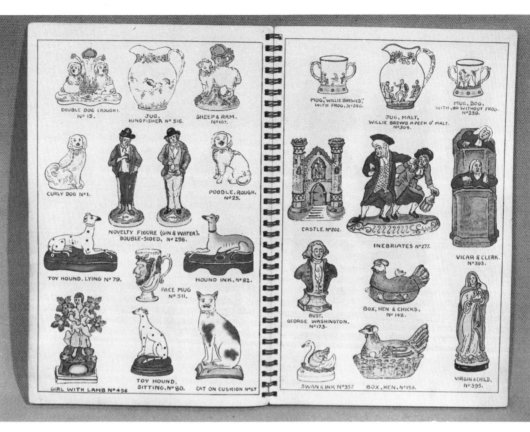

DOUBLE DOG (ROUGH). No 15.

JUG. KINGFISHER No 516.

SHEEP & RAM. No 107.

CURLY DOG No 1.

NOVELTY FIGURE (GIN & WATER). DOUBLE-SIDED, No 258.

POODLE, ROUGH. No 25.

TOY HOUND, LYING No 79.

FACE MUG No 511.

HOUND INK, No 82.

GIRL WITH LAMB No 456.

TOY HOUND, SITTING, No 80.

CAT ON CUSHION No 67.

MUG, "WILLIE BREWED," WITH FROG, No 240.

JUG, MALT, WILLIE BREWD A PECK O' MALT. No 304.

MUG, DOG, WITH, OR WITHOUT FROG. No 239.

CASTLE, No 202.

INEBRIATES No 277.

VICAR & CLERK. No 393.

BUST, GEORGE WASHINGTON. No 173.

BOX, HEN & CHICKS, No 142.

SWAN & INK No 357.

BOX, HEN, No 159.

VIRGIN & CHILD, No 395.

HEARTY GOODFELLOW No 373.

SQUIRE No 380.

SNUFFTAKER No 390.

JUDY No 382.

ORDINARY No 387.

PUNCH No 381.

JUDY CREAM JUG No 315.

TOBY TEAPOT No 366.

PUNCH CREAM JUG No 315.

TOBY MUG, No 368.

JOLLY MILLER No 370.

WATCHMAN No 464.

SOUTER JOHNNY

SOUTER JOHNNY No 470.

TAM SHANTER

TAM O SHANTER No 471.

PICKWICK No 391.

FIGURE, SHOEBLACK No 345.

JOHN BULL No 374.

DEER HUNTERS Nº 211.

FRENCH FRUIT SELLER Nº 218.

SMALL TOBY, (KNEELING) Nº 481.

SAILORS FAREWELL Nº 348.

SMALL TOBY, (MAN) Nº 481.

SCHOOL BOY & GIRL, NESTING, Nº 337.

FLOWER GIRL Nº 233.

SCOTCH DANCERS Nº 559.

FRUIT SELLER (WOMAN) Nº 228.

CRINOLINE Nº 165.

FRUIT SELLER (MAN) Nº 228.

NEWS GIRL Nº 187.

SOLDIERS FAREWELL Nº 348.

CROSSING SWEEPER Nº 187.

COW & MILKMAID (PAIR) Nº 62.

PRINCE & PRINCESS (PAIR) Nº 316.

DONKEY Nº 73.

HOUND & HARE (PAIR) Nº 85.

SPANIEL, SITTING, (PR.) Nº 32.

ZEBRA, (PAIR) Nº 113.

VINTAGE REAPER (PAIR) Nº 394.

COW CREAM (NO STAND) Nº 60.

PARROT (PAIR) Nº 102.

COACH DOG, SITTING, (PR) Nº 14.

KENTS "OLD STAFFORDSHIRE" POTTERY IS
NOT "REPRODUCTION" IN THE STRICTEST
SENSE OF THE WORD, BECAUSE, EXCEPT
FOR A PERIOD DURING WARTIME, THE
POTTERY HAS BEEN PRODUCED CONTIN-
UOUSLY FROM THE EARLY DAYS.

WE, WHO APPRECIATE THESE EXAMPLES
OF A PERIOD IN STAFFORDSHIRE POTTERY
HAVE TO THANK MEMBERS OF THE KENT
FAMILY FOR PRESERVING THE MANUFAC-
TURE OF TRADITIONAL POTTERY AT THE
EXPENSE OF MODERN DEVELOPMENT.

THE AUTHOR—1955.

SEE LIST AT END OF BOOKLET.

WILLIAM KENT (Porcelains) LTD.,

AUCKLAND STREET,

BURSLEM, ENGLAND.

111. M'Grath and Pretender. Greyhound rivals for the Waterloo Cup. *c.*1871. 10 ins.

poor, since by the time Victoria came to the throne the enclosure of land by farmers and private landowners was virtually complete. A well trained whippet could evade a gamekeeper where his master ran the risk of prison or being caught in a jagged-toothed steel man trap. So the dogs made by the potters are not, as thought by many collectors, coursing greyhounds with hares but whippets with rabbits, and indeed if you look closely at the prey you will see quite clearly that they have the shorter ears and back legs of the rabbit. The workers raced their whippets against each other, too. Perhaps they still do, certainly as a child in the 1930s I used to watch the Welsh miners racing them to a distant waving handkerchief on the hillsides of my youth. The greyhound was the true racing and coursing dog and there are two very rare titled figures of the famous black greyhound Master M'Grath who won The Waterloo Cup in 1868–69 and '71 when he defeated a light brown dog called Pretender. Master M'Grath was the most famous greyhound who ever lived. His name was celebrated in popular songs and ballads and Queen Victoria summoned him to appear before her at Windsor. (111)

Some of the finest whippets and rabbit pairs were made about 1855. They often have fine underglaze black spots with bases coloured in a distinctive shade of turquoise blue. This greeny-blue and the simple gold motif seen in Figure 112 is also found on figures made during the Crimean War.

Many of the eighteenth century animal figures and groups are now beyond the means of the average collector but there is a vast field to choose from in those made in the nineteenth century. Above all, the Victorians made more of them and they were

112. Whippets and
rabbits. *c*.1855. 11 ins.

113. Circus equestrienne. Typical
of many such acts in the
travelling fairgrounds. *c*.1850.
8½ ins.

114. Often said to be the famous Andrew Ducrow and his wife Louisa Woolford. This pair could equally represent many similar circus acts of the day. *c.*1850. 10 ins.

more truly English in spirit. If you can afford a fortune and long for a pair of Whieldon buffaloes mounted by oriental children made about 1760, then a fortune you will certainly have to pay. But their charm is academic, they were an attempt to emulate the pottery and porcelain imported from China and Germany, whereas the exotic beasts potted in the nineteenth century were imported themselves in the flesh. They were not sploshing around in far distant rice paddies to appear at third hand in English clay, they could be seen by every lady and gentleman for a shilling and every working man for sixpence. They touched a spring in the art of naïve potting in England which had never been tapped before. They are as English as the gentle, comforting pairs of spaniels and the sporting whippets whose mantel-shelves they so often shared.

5
Cottages, Castles
and Pastille Burners

The first Public Health Act in England dates from 1848. It was passed as a panic measure to combat outbreaks of cholera and was largely ineffective. Not until the building and sanitary reforms of the 1870s did the death rate show a marked fall.

When England was largely a rural community in the eighteenth century, drainage and sanitation had been just as bad. The water closet was a novel rarity and most lavatories were simply either deep pits in the gardens of the middle classes, or enclosed boxes in the houses of the rich. Such conditions were accepted as an inevitable fact of nature and were tolerable in the low density population of the villages, and in country houses which were only too well ventilated by every breeze that blew and served by cheap domestic labour to carry water and empty the slops. Even the towns were not jam-packed with humanity such as we have seen happened in the nineteenth century. The overcrowding in the slum dwellings for workers then was appalling, with many of them literally living over cess pits under the floor boards.

In effect, from the late years of the eighteenth century urban England became smellier and smellier until by the 1850s it stank to the skies. No wonder there was a passion for wild country scenery far from the stews of the towns, where clean winds blessed the nose and rivers and streams were bright and pure. In earlier ages sweet smelling herbs had been strewn on floors, but in Victorian times although the cry of "Buy my Sweet Lavender" was heard all over the towns and cities something more effective was needed to make life tolerable.

It wasn't only the lavatories. Middle-class terraced town houses were built tall and narrow with kitchens in the basement for cooking endless gargantuan meals for large families with almost as many servants to wait on them. With poor ventilation the hot air from the coal-fired ovens had to rise up through the house, pausing only to pick up the stench from the earth closets, commodes and chamber pots on the way. In fact, even earth closets didn't come into use until 1860 and they were a rarity inside the house, most of them were banished to the bottom of the garden and for indoor sanitation people relied on chamber pots and commodes. The water closet had been invented much earlier but did not come into general use until the 1880s.

For the poor labouring classes the foul air surrounding them became an accepted fact of life, like the piles of human manure and rotting garbage in the mean and narrow alleys of their slums. Only gradually did the middle classes rebel against it and then more from fear of disease than anything else. There was deep distrust of reform, which they saw as state interference with the liberty of the citizen to live as he liked however noxious his surroundings.

These were the conditions which accounted for the great popularity of the nineteenth century pastille burners which have become so popular with collectors in recent years.

First of all, let us start with a pastille itself. There were numerous commercial variations of these, or ladies so inclined could make them from their own recipes. The idea was to try and sweeten the room and if there seemed no hope of getting rid of the source, the obvious plan would be to drown the bad smell with something sweet and scented. The strewn herbs of Elizabethan days crushed underfoot on the stone flags to release the soft palliatives of thyme and marjoram were no longer practical or powerful enough. A slow burning trickle of strongly scented smoke worked better and lasted longer. The pastilles were small cones of various combinations of ingredients, the most common of which seem to have been finely powdered charcoal made from willow twigs combined with benzoin, which was an aromatic resin imported from Java, or any concentrated perfumed oil bound together and pinched into a cone shape with gum arabic.

When lit the pastille would glow and smoulder for a considerable time giving off a thin stream of heavily perfumed smoke rising into the room through the miniature chimneys of the little cottages, houses or castles called pastille burners. They are found occasionally from the early eighteenth century in slipware, crudely decorated with trickles of different coloured liquid clay. Unlike the early figures and animals of the same period they don't fetch very high prices even though they are quite rare, mainly I suspect because they are basically dumpy and unattractive. Later, a few appeared about 1750 made in the style of the Whieldon school, hand modelled in the likeness of half-timbered cottages and decorated with mingled tortoise-shell glazes – these are difficult to find and expensive.

There exist some early records of public auctions for the soft paste porcelain products of the famous Chelsea factory. A sixteen-day sale in 1756, however, mentions only two pieces which might have been pastille burners. Both were described as: "A most beautiful perfume pot in the form of an old castle or pigeon house decorated with pigeons". I have not been able to establish a date at which pastilles were first made and in general use although, of course, incense was well known in many parts of the Empire. It seems more likely that "perfume pot" meant a container for dried herbs and flower heads, a pot-pourri in fact. Chelsea porcelain always commands high prices which average collectors cannot easily afford, but it is worth mentioning these two pigeon houses or castles since they would seem to be in shape and form the early prototypes of the pastille burner of the nineteenth century.

115. Early pastille burner in the form of a *cottage ornée* showing the sliding tray for holding the scented charcoal cones. Porcelain. *c.*1825. 6 ins.

The huge output of the decorated castles and cottages which are more readily available to collectors, coincides in direct proportion with the population explosion in the towns of the Industrial Revolution and the introduction and general use of the new hard paste porcelain bodies or bone china after 1800. Similarly it declined towards the end of the century as local government slowly became an effective power in the land and the air became sweeter.

Pastille burners were made in a great variety of shapes and forms but basically their design was dictated by the need for a free flow of air over the smouldering pastille to ensure steady and continuous combustion. This, in the simplest examples, was achieved by placing the pastille on a small indentation on the base of the structure which was surmounted by a pierced upper section which could either be lifted off to give easy access or was an integral part of the whole, when the pastille could be placed in position through an aperture at the back. More complicated forms had small trays which could be slid into the interior of the burner. (115) In some examples the roof and the walls were made in one piece and in others the roof, walls and base were all separate and could be assembled to make up the whole without any obvious joins. (116) All cottages with separate units are a nightmare for antique dealers to display safely. Unless they are confined to the closed cabinets, casual browsers have been known to panic when they pick one up by the roof and find the whole piece apparently disintegrating in their hands. More than one attractive burner has been dropped and damaged beyond repair in this way. Dealers will always appreciate a customer who

116. When assembled these three sections form the bone china burner shown in Figure 122.

asks first if he may pick something up and examine it. Such browsers frequently come into the category I call J.L.s or J.P.s – (Just Looking or Just Pricing). Genuine collectors are no problem because they are well aware of the dangers but J.P.s and J.L.s can be a menace.

The pastille burner first came to be made in quantity about 1820. The earliest examples were very fine with a wealth of decoration. Some were much larger than the ones which were made in the 1830s and '40s. These early cottages were made from quite thick heavy porcelain so that frequently there was some difficulty in the process of manufacture. Firing cracks can be seen on many of them. These were easily disguised by the rich application of encrusted decoration, flowers or trailing ivy conveniently following the line of the firing flaw on walls and on the grassy mounds on which the building sat. The entire underside of the base of Figure 115 has been laboriously painted to simulate marble to disguise quite a heavy firing crack. It has not been added later but was done at the time it was made. These ornate early burners had a sliding tray sometimes big enough to accommodate two or even three pastilles, and were of a quality which suggests that they were made for the upper end of the market; they wouldn't have been cheap even when they were made. They are so unlike any of the other designs both contemporary and those which followed, that I began to suspect that they were based on illustrations which the potters had seen and worked from and yet it seemed odd that any real houses or cottages could ever have existed in such a profuse and elaborate mixture of architectural design. Tudor chimneys thrust through thatched roofs over walls with gothic windows looking out on to gardens which belong to the pages of children's fairytale books or seed catalogues.

I was, therefore, intrigued and delighted to discover that such rural fantasies had not only been designed by such famous architects as John Nash but that they had been built in considerable numbers in the first quarter of the nineteenth century for rich and aristocratic patrons who, like Marie Antoinette before them, had felt an urge to return to nature. It was, of course, a most unnatural nature but there they were – and in a few rare survivals – still are; the ridiculous but completely charming *cottages ornées* like the Swiss Cottage Cahir or the most elaborate one of all, The Royal Lodge in Windsor Great Park which Nash designed for George IV. The popularity of the *cottage ornée* coincides exactly with the production of the early ornate fantasy pastille burners and there can be no doubt that in them, through contemporary illustrations, lies the potters' source of inspiration. They are quite different from the burners which we shall see in a moment were based on the little summer houses and gazebos. They are bigger and more ornate and yet obviously real houses disguised as cottages. One has to say disguised for what cottage ever had fourteen bedrooms hung with Chinese wallpaper, as some of these did when Nash built them.

Judging by the fine workmanship and design these burners were made about 1820–30 and were never aimed at the lower end of the market. It was a luxury trade and only later in the century did cheaper designs begin to appear. (115, 117–19)

Contemporary with the heavy porcelain *cottages ornées* were some smaller, more delicately potted cottages. Their main feature was the thin bone china construction often in two or more sections, with encrustations of paper-thin flowers, roses, tulips, morning glory and the newly introduced dahlias. Occasionally nestling among the flowers there are small plump fruits, miniature melons or acorns, a profusion of plenty with a splendid disregard for shape, size or season. The new town people had a decidedly romantic view of a country cottage. It had become a symbol for them of a way of life they had lost, you can find the theme perpetuated by painters throughout the Victorian age. The working classes remembered Walton's plump fleecy sheep but those above them never remembered the broken down shambles that agricultural labourers tolerated. For them every country cottage was a rustic dream with roses always in full bloom around the door.

Like their ornate cottage contemporaries these flower cottages were very fine. There were fewer firing cracks because they were mostly more thinly potted and the flowers are really quite remarkable in their delicacy. Most of the petals have long since been damaged by clumsy handling although occasionally one comes across a superb specimen which has survived almost intact, probably because it has always been kept in a display cabinet. Don't be put off by a few petal chips, perfect specimens are few and far between. Don't wait for them; you may be passing by good early examples which will not come your way at that price again. All pastille burners have increased in price over the last ten years and on average this increase has been proportionally greater than for other collectors' items.

Three other main influences on design appear in the early period: Greek classical architecture, the Chinese style made popular by the splendid excesses of the Prince Regent at Brighton Pavilion, and the Gothic style inspired by one of its earliest revivals.

117–119. Three sides of the same *cottage ornée* showing the great care and attention to detail in the design and decoration of these rare early burners. Porcelain. *c.*1825. 6 ins.

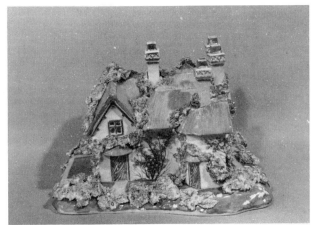

93

120. Bone china. *c*.1830. 6 ins.   121. Bone china. *c*.1835. 5½ ins.

All these had some impact on landscape garden design and many of the purely decorative gazebos, summer houses and follies in the planned landscapes of the great country houses bear a striking likeness to some of the early pastille burners. If the evidence of the potters' sources of inspiration for their figures is considered, then it seems quite possible that some of these classical and oriental designs may well have been influenced by the shapes of the little decorative conceits appearing in the country gardens of the new industrial rich. (124–126) Nor were the designs confined to fantasy, there are some churches too, just as lavishly encrusted with flowers, those with turrets and the ones with elegant spires are both rare and tend to be expensive.

From the evidence of the potting, the numerous castle shapes both representative and imaginative appear to come a little later in time, about 1830 onwards. A castle design which appears more than any other can be seen in Figure 127. This can be positively identified as Warwick Castle and its popularity and relative nearness to Staffordshire must have attracted the potters for it turns up over and over again in various colours, peach, white and lilac, sometimes the shape of the castle is left plain but many examples are heavily flowered and gilded, with the turrets fringed with green or white shreds of clay to look like ivy or moss.

94

122. It is rare to find the flower petals in such fine condition as this. Bone china. *c.*1830. 6½ ins.

123. Farmhouse in bone china. *c.*1835. 6 ins.

124. The Prince Regent's oriental taste spread from Brighton and for many years influenced garden follies, gazebos and pastille burners. Lilac-coloured bone china. *c.*1845. 10½ ins.

125. A pottery burner by Thomas Parr based on a gothic garden gazebo. *c.*1852. 6 ins.

95

126. A triple burner in lilac bone china. Also found in white. c.1848. 7¾ ins.

127. Warwick Castle. Lilac bone china. c.1850. 6¾ ins.

96

128. Porcelain burners. *c.*1850. 4½ ins.

129. Pottery burners. *c.*1850. 5 ins.

So far the cottages and castles we have been considering were almost without exception made for the more elegant market of the middle classes and were made with some care and attention to detail in fine quality bone china porcelain. From the late 1840s onwards more and more pottery pastille burners were made alongside those of porcelain. Sometimes identical designs can be found in both bodies. From the crudeness of the modelling and decoration it would seem that they were aimed at a much cheaper market. Probably their appeal was not due to any increased sensitivity in the noses of the poor working class people who could now afford them. More likely they were attracted by the charm of the elegant little porcelain fantasies they would

97

130. James Blomfield
Rush 1800–1849,
murderer and auctioneer.
Conducted his own
defence and is seen here
making his final abortive
defence speech which
lasted for over fourteen
hours. c.1849. 10 ins.

have seen while working as servants in the grand houses of their employers. (128)

There is some evidence to support this theory for after a while, about 1860, the openings to insert the pastilles are often omitted from the design although frequently such openings were still indicated in the mould at the back by a slight indentation like a blank door. This was the beginning of quite a different style of cottages, houses and castles. They no longer served a practical purpose but were made for exactly the same popular market which bought portrait figures of the famous personalities of the day.

The Staffordshire potters were above all commercial to their clever finger tips; they had to be. If their products didn't sell they were out of work. Art for art's sake was not for them, their sole aim was to supply their customers with what they wanted and if they wanted to know all the gory details of the latest murder and to buy a pottery house of the scene of the crime the potters were happy to supply them.

In 1849 James Blomfield Rush was hanged in public on the bridge over the moat at Norwich Castle. Rush had owned Potash Farm but had mortgaged it for £5,000 to Isaac Jermy, the Recorder of Norwich and Rush's neighbour, who lived a mile away at Stanfield Hall. The mortgage fell due at midnight on November 30th, 1848 but, with the impulsiveness of a bad chess player gambling on a quick solution to the mess on the board, Rush entered the Hall at 8.00 p.m. on the evening of November 28th. He shot Jermy and his son dead and wounded the son's wife and the maid. He had forged Jermy's signature to a document which purported to give him the complete ownership of Potash Farm.

The public were fascinated and the potters had a field day producing not only figures of Rush and his mistress Emily Sandford whose evidence had hanged him, but also portrait houses of both Potash Farm and Stanfield Hall. (130, 131) There is at least one

131. Potash Farm and Stanfield Hall. *c.*1849. 8½, 8 ins.

accurately titled model of Norwich Castle which is suitably now in the Castle Museum at Norwich. There are occasionally found other castle figures titled "Norwich Castle" but these titles were applied by the potters to an existing castle mould which bears no resemblance to the real castle. It was a quick way of cashing in on a nine-days wonder.

In 1854 William Palmer, a member of the Royal College of Surgeons, was in general practice in the county town of Rugely in Staffordshire. In that same year he poisoned his wife. In 1855 he poisoned his brother and his best friend. General practice had begun to assume a more sinister meaning in Rugely until Palmer was arrested, tried and hanged in June 1856. Palmer lived in a typical plain Georgian house which the potters reproduced faithfully and titled "Palmer's House" in large, raised capital letters. (132, 133)

Accurate portraits of titled castles appear in the 1860s and '70s and probably were sold to tourists who, through the spread of the railway system, were able to visit them for the first time; among them, Beaumaris, Caernarvon, Dudley, Balmoral, Scarborough and Windsor. The railway itself is represented in a portrait of Euston Station which opened in 1848. Although untitled it is easily identified by the delightful railway train and the beautiful Doric entrance arch which remained until the station was vandalized in 1963. Less identifiable are the buildings titled "St Roch" and "Brunswick School", although there must have been a market for them at the time. Perhaps they were ordered as special commissions in a limited edition, for this was done in the case of other figures I have researched. There is no doubt that the titled "Trinity College" was made to commemorate the Prince of Wales's attendance there on June 18th, 1861. (134)

99

132. William Palmer 1824–1856, member of the Royal College of Surgeons and poisoner. Hanged June 1856. *c*.1856. 11¼ ins.

133. Palmer's House in Rugeley from a print in *The Illustrated London News*. *c*.1856. 7½ ins.

This then was the main progression in the style and types of the small decorated buildings in the nineteenth century, all of which are now much sought after and collected. Firstly, the early elaborate heavy porcelain and the delicate flower encrusted bone china, moving on through the century until quite a large number have lost their original purpose and have become purely decorative, or commemorative pottery or porcelain cottages and castles. Some collectors place an exaggerated value on lilac-coloured pastille burners and they can be very attractive, although in my experience not nearly so rare as many people think. I have seen one with what could be a Minton date mark for 1855 but it didn't look much like Minton's style; safer to call it Staffordshire porcelain even though I believe it was made at about that date, as were I think many of the lilac burners. At least it had some quality, unlike the little horror shown in Figure 135 which is poor quality and quite modern. The flowers are like the lumpy sugar decorations sold to decorate Christmas cakes, the leaves are thick with crude, heavy veining and the broad gold line round the base has been rubbed away at the time it was made to suggest age.

There is another group of cottages and houses which developed from the pastille burner and had a quite separate practical purpose. These are little money boxes which are similar to the more robust pottery burners of the 1850s and '60s, except of course they are moulded as a closed box shape with only a slit for the coin in the roof. I have never seen one with any provision made for extracting the money, so perhaps they were meant to encourage thrift. Sometimes the coin slit is broken, mute evidence of some little boy's or girl's attempt to repossess the trapped riches with the aid of a table knife. A popular money box was produced with two little guardian figures on either side of it. They were nearly always made in high-temperature underglaze Pratt-ware, a style of

134. The Great Gate of Trinity
College, Cambridge. *c*.1861. 8 ins.

135. Fake burner in the form of a
dovecote. Lilac porcelain. *c*.1975. 4 ins.

136. Money box. *c*.1840. 6¾ ins.

137. Cottages from the Kent catalogue 1960. The "Man Cottage", bottom centre, was well coloured in the Pratt style and is often sold as genuine. *c*.1960. 4¾ ins.

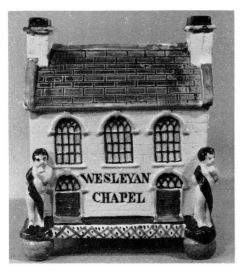

138. Money box. *c*.1840. 6¾ ins.

potting which first appeared in the late eighteenth century. This is probably the reason why they are so often given too early a date. The style of the architecture, however, puts them firmly into the nineteenth century and because many of them were ordered for individual children it is possible to say that they seem to have been produced from about 1840 with similar examples dated as late as 1862. These handsome Pratt-style money boxes are usually about 6¾ inches high and supported on ball feet. (136) Collectors should be very wary of a much smaller version about 4¾ inches high and guarded by two little men or a man and a woman. There are little faces to be seen in the upper windows. These are almost always modern reproductions and may be seen in far too many sale-rooms and antique shops. (137)

The genuine ones bearing a child's name and sometimes the date were probably given as christening presents. There is new evidence to support this which is interesting, in that it is the first time I have found documentary proof not only to support the christening present theory but to indicate the social background of the family that bought it for their child.

Although the money box bearing the inscription "Mary Ann Goodhand Lincoln" is undated, a search in the archives of Lincoln revealed that she was born on July 3rd, 1840, the daughter of James Goodhand, a labourer, and his wife Bridget who signed the birth certificate with a cross. Only two years and eight months later a death certificate shows that the child died of typhoid. Poor little mite, she didn't have long to save her pennies and there would have been very few of them anyway. A labourer's wage in 1840 was very low, that and her mother's illiteracy and indeed the disease which killed the child so young suggest a background of poverty. Yes, it does establish the background and that is important evidence, but sometimes research can seem a little like prying. (136)

This same model was used for other special commissions and appears with the name of a charity school or a Wesleyan Chapel. (138) One of the most important days of a child's life in those days was the Sunday School Anniversary. They paraded the streets with banners and assembled in the chapel to sing in patiently rehearsed children's choirs or, if a child had a retentive memory, to give suitable recitations. There were races and sports if a field could still be found and I don't doubt that the anniversaries would explain the popularity of these little pottery chapels.

How do I know about chapel anniversaries? Well, there are good contemporary accounts which I have read with instant sympathy and recognition; for, gentle reader, I was myself brought up in a Welsh mining valley as a very Primitive Methodist and I've seen it and done it all, including my first appearance in public, rendering a poem. It was far too long and I dried stone cold half way through it; I never heard the promptings of my agonized mother, all I know was that I had never seen so many faces *en masse* before. I can't remember the name of the poem, only the line on which I dried: "And I shall *spit*, like the man that digs the garden". Perhaps as a little boy of four I felt then, as I certainly do now, that it was rather an unsuitable poem for a chapel anniversary, anyway I never got a pottery chapel as a prize.

Who made pastille burners? Well, the vast majority were made in Staffordshire and bear no factory mark so that it is very difficult to assign a particular specimen to a specific factory. Sometimes a piece will show so many features in common with one of the rare marked examples as to make it virtually certain that it comes from the same factory, but even this method can present problems. I have seen what appeared to be two identical cottages one clearly and authentically marked Spode (139) and its twin bearing an equally genuine CD mark in underglaze blue which would place it as coming from the Coalport factory in Shropshire.

Although at first sight these cottage pastille burners appeared to be identical there were in fact slight differences in basic design. The Spode cottage was on a slightly higher mound, so that there were twice as many steps leading up to the door. But they were so very alike that had one of them not been marked it would have been understandable to have ascribed them to the same factory.

The Spode factory was succeeded in 1833 by Copeland and Garrett until 1847 and was continued thereafter by Copeland alone. The Spode pastille burner remained in production and examples marked both Copeland and Garrett and finally Copeland are known, although neither of these was as fine as the original Spode or the Coalport.

Considering that pastille burners were so popular and that so many of them were made, it's strange that so very few of them bear a factory mark. There have been recorded marked examples by Minton, Coalport, Spode, Copeland and Garrett, Copeland, Flight Barr and Barr of Worcester and Chamberlain's Worcester; I have also heard of, but not seen, others marked Barr Flight and Barr.

Why the myth of the Rockingham cottage has become so established it is difficult to say, but the fact remains that many people, some of them dealers, persist in perpetuating it. Even some comparatively recent magazine articles have been embarrassingly detailed in their description of the wholly imaginary characteristics of Rockingham pastille burners. Such articles are without a word of truth in them. One day a complete pastille burner cottage or castle with a genuine Rockingham factory mark may appear but until then it must be accepted that the Rockingham factory was not responsible for the huge number of cottages and castles with which both dealers and collectors have mistakenly associated it for so many years.

Any collector would be delighted to have some factory marked examples but I know of magnificent collections with not one marked piece in them. I have no doubt that the great majority of these little cottages and castles, both pottery and porcelain, were made in the hundreds of small anonymous factories that flourished in the Staffordshire pottery area. They vary enormously in quality and design but they nearly all have something to commend them, even though it is unlikely that we shall ever discover where and by whom most of them were made. (140)

139. Porcelain burner marked Spode. *c.*1820. $4\frac{1}{2}$ ins.

140. A selection of cottages, castles and money boxes. *c.*1820–1860.

141. Dudley
Castle. *c.*1850.
6¼ ins

142. Beaumaris
Castle. *c.*1850.
6¼ ins.

143. Caernarvon Castle. *c.*1850. 7½ ins.

144. Windsor Castle. *c*.1850. 6 ins.

In a way I have always thought this to have distinct advantages for the collector. If that seems at first a strange thing to say, I can explain. There is, I believe, a great danger in what I can only call mark mania. It leads collectors, or some of them, to seek marked pieces to the exclusion of all other considerations. A mark has interest but it is not the most important thing to look for. It may accompany quality and artistry but it cannot guarantee it. The true value and merit lie in the piece itself and not in the mark underneath it. There is no short cut to taste and appreciation, they come by learning to use one's eyes and by comparing the workmanship of one piece with another; the design itself, the delicacy and colouring of the flowers or the infinite care with which some painter long ago outlined the veins on a leaf. They are born of enthusiasm more than scholarship and pedantry. Taken to extremes mark mania is sad – like ignoring the Venus de Milo in the Louvre because she hasn't got Copeland or Minton stamped on her bum.

The superb early burner, the *cottage ornée* in the centre of Colour Plate III has been through a major London sale-room at least twice in the last fifteen years. It bears a Spode mark on the base for 1820, and was catalogued as such. I'm quite sure it is Spode, too, for it has many characteristics in common with other marked Spode burners of that date. The interesting thing is that the mark is a forgery painted on over the glaze. Now the piece is just as splendid with or without that mark, but it does show the lengths to which some unscrupulous people will go to satisfy this unnecessary passion for marks.

107

As with all things sought by collectors there are entire pastille burners which have been produced expressly to deceive. Some of them are quite ambitious with flower and moss encrustations very similar to those found on some of early period porcelain burners, but close examination will show that they have been made quickly and without that careful attention to detail which distinguishes the originals. They cannot be confused with the modern reproductions of the present Coalport factory which are very well made and clearly marked. William Kent, too, reproduced many of the early pastille burners made originally by Thomas Parr in the 1850s. These, however, were not marked by Kent and have caused some troubles for collectors (137). Until a collector has learned what to look for he should confine his early buys to those pieces sold by a reputable and knowledgeable dealer, bearing in mind that those two attributions are not necessarily always found together. Experience can be expensive but need not be so. A good dealer may well charge what he believes is the true current market value but with his guarantee he is cheap in the long run.

Considering their great popularity, both at the time they were made and with collectors today, it is surprising that so little has been written about pastille burners. References to them as articles in use are almost non-existent in contemporary literature, possibly because they were so commonly accepted as a necessary part of everyday life, and similarly, apart from a few rare marked specimens in specialist books, modern writers have largely ignored them. Their charm and importance is not concerned with the factory which may or may not have made them. They are a social comment. They are about people and the way they lived and people are always more important than marks.

145. The Elementary Education
Act of 1870. 7¼ ins.

✤ 6 ✤
John and Rebecca Lloyd
of Shelton

It's a great temptation, especially for new collectors, to think of style in potting as belonging to fixed, immovable periods of time. It does at first make the overall picture a little easier to understand but such over-simplification can in the long run give an inaccurate view.

Styles influenced each other less than might be expected and when new potters came along their figures and groups were produced side by side with those of an earlier generation. Many books which cover the different styles of figure making in the nineteenth century graze contentedly over pretty much the same pastures and the reader is led fairly accurately, if sometimes unimaginatively, from the late productions of the Woods through Sherratt and the Walton school until with more than a hint of nose wrinkling they are pushed into a ditch full of flat-back figures in the 1840s and '50s. Balston, Pugh and Haggar are obvious exceptions, of course, because they write of Staffordshire figures with experience and knowledge. Haggar did a superb job in unearthing the work of hitherto unknown potters, and yet even in these three authors there is one important group of figures which has been for all practical purposes ignored completely.

In my first book, *The Victorian Staffordshire Figure*, I discussed this group of figures and identified them as appearing with certainty round about 1820 and continuing in production up to and into the early years of Victoria's reign.

Now, more than ten years later seems a good time to discuss them more fully. They were, above all, superbly modelled and of a very fine quality white porcelain body. They were often, but by no means always, given passages of deep cobalt underglaze blue which was to become such a feature of the later Victorian figures. The gilding where it occurred was often rich and generous. They were modelled in the round so they could be viewed from all sides. They used a firm, simple base which could be square or round with a short support to give the piece strength and stability when the subject was standing. Seated subjects were sometimes modelled on suitably moulded bases and all of them without exception were made with great attention to detail. What I had not realized when I first recorded them was that far more were made than I had suspected and that quite a number of them were portraits. These are indeed the true forerunners of that wonderful flood of portrait figures which came from the Staffordshire potteries in the Victorian period. Some of those Victorian figures were of a very high quality but with the commercial pressure on the potters to increase production to supply the greater demand, design became more and more economical until later in the century many of them were made from a simple two-piece mould. The fact that the potters became marvellously clever in adapting to this enforced simplicity worked to our advantage because it virtually forced them into a new form of primitive art which is only now being fully recognized and appreciated. But it was very different from this early group of porcelain portraits which we are discussing here.

So fine are they and of such quality and sophistication that paradoxically I believe this to be the main reason they have been passed over almost without mention by ceramic historians, and when they found their way into collections – sometimes even those owned by serious research workers – they were wrongly attributed to Rockingham or nineteenth century Derby simply because it was not thought possible for such fine figures to have been made in Staffordshire. This in spite of the fact that the figure productions of both those factories were all documented and researched and that their figures, almost without exception, were clearly marked or numbered with a factory code on the base, whereas these early Staffordshire figures were rarely marked.

Again the Rockingham myth dies hardest of all, especially among collectors of theatrical figures. Any fine quality porcelain figure which is obviously, or could be conceivably, a portrait of a theatre personality is claimed as Rockingham. Now the fact is that the Rockingham list includes only seven theatre portraits. They have all been positively identified beyond any doubt or question. They are all portraits of one man; the comedian John Liston in some of his most famous roles. Why Rockingham only made theatre figures of John Liston and of no other actor I do not know but that is the fact. Incidentally, in case future researchers may be confused I should point out that there is a mistake in the Rockingham list of figures in the books so far published. They all list model No. 6 as Madame Vestris singing *Buy a Broom*. It is an understandable slip since that was indeed one of her most famous and successful songs. Poor Madame Vestris! She would not have been pleased to see Liston's lugubrious and unmistakable features listed as a portrait of her beautiful face. There are accurate ceramic portraits of her as the Broom Girl but the Rockingham figure is Liston's portrait, exactly as he looked when he appeared with her dressed in that identical costume.

Madame sang this song for the first time for Liston's benefit performance at the Theatre Royal, Haymarket, on September 18th, 1826 and the Rockingham portrait was copied faithfully from a print lithograph published by Ingrey and Madeley in that same year. It shows Vestris and Liston dressed exactly alike singing *The Broom Girl* as a duet. (146, 147)

It is quite true that the Rockingham list may well not be complete and it is possible that other figures may be discovered in the future. Nevertheless, on the evidence we have so far, it is reasonable to assume that if they do they will be as clearly marked or titled as are the ones we already know. Certainly there can be no justification for the

146. A marked Rockingham porcelain portrait figure of John Liston as a Broom Girl. *c.*1826. 6¼ ins.

147. The source for Figure 146. Crown Copyright Victoria and Albert Museum.

great numbers of figures which are claimed as Rockingham. I am now less optimistic than I used to be when I first tried to explode the Rockingham myth. In my innocence I believed then that both dealers and collectors would abandon their claims but this has not happened. I suppose it is understandable that some dealers with few scruples or scant knowledge should wish to attribute a piece to Rockingham, for that factory made some superb quality porcelain portrait figures, and since they were probably only produced for a very limited period – from 1826 to 1830 – they are extremely rare and much sought after. But it seems odd that specialist collectors who often know more than some dealers should still be so determined to deceive themselves.

There are fewer claims made for Derby but then the factory produced figures for a far longer period and they are not nearly as rare. There is an interesting but unproven connection between the Derby and Rockingham factories. After a close examination of all the relevant figures I believe it most probable that the Rockingham Liston figures were designed by the Derby modeller of both Liston and Vestris, Samuel Keys Jnr. There is some difficulty in this because early accounts record him as still working at Derby until 1830, yet the visual evidence is so strong as to suggest that either he left earlier with his brother Edward in 1826, or that he modelled the Liston figures for Rockingham before he left Derby. Whatever the truth of the matter, and we may never

149. The impressed mark of John and Rebecca Lloyd of Shelton.

148. The Lloyds at their best; superb modelling full of movement and spirit, generous gold band on the base. Probably a portrait from a print of Thomas Potter Cooke. *c.*1835. 9 ins.

now be certain, I shall always see his very individual style in all the figures of John Liston made at the Rockingham factory.

It is much more certain that when the Keys brothers left Derby they were both soon employed in the Staffordshire potteries, and this could have some significance when we come to speculate on the possible origin of some of our unidentified porcelain portrait figures.

First, I think we should ask ourselves if they could be attributed to any one factory and I think the answer should be no. They all share common features, fine careful modelling, a good white porcelainous body and extreme attention to detail; delicate faces, eyes and eyebrows and often a delight of movement in the human figure portrayed. After that it must be said that they vary considerably in the style of decoration and gilding so as to make it seem unlikely that they all come from the same factory. The most that can be said is that there were factories producing such figures in Staffordshire in the early decades of the nineteenth century and that until now they

150. The Tipsy Lawyer, The Italian Boy and The Little Farm Girl. Lloyd. *c*.1835. 5, 4, 4¼ ins.

151. Shepherd and Shepherdess. Impressed Lloyd Shelton examples are known. *c*.1840. 5, 5½ ins.

have been underestimated and indeed largely ignored.

There are two reasons for believing that they all originate in Staffordshire. The first is not so easy to explain but after many years of handling the figures of that area it is difficult not to develop an instinct about it, just as one does about Derby or Rockingham, and all of them have qualities which convince me that they are Staffordshire. The second reason is more definite in that one distinctive group of figures which all came from the same factory are occasionally stamped with the mark of John and Rebecca Lloyd of Shelton, in the heart of the potteries.

Their most active period of production seems to have been from about 1834–50 and only a relatively small number of their figures bear the mark LLOYD/SHELTON either on the back or underneath. I have tried to discover more about the Lloyds but even with the kind help of Arnold Mountford, the Director of Museums in Stoke-on-Trent, I have learned no more than Haggar tells us in a few lines. To these meagre facts he adds that they made flat-back figures, but most of the Lloyd figures I have seen have been moulded in the round. True, they were fond of placing seated figures in chairs with plain undecorated backs like Tam o'Shanter and Souter Johnny but I have never seen a true flat-back Lloyd-Shelton. (148–157)

It is always difficult to describe colour accurately in words and even the best photographic colour reproduction may be inconsistent and unreliable, but the Lloyd-Shelton figures were carefully decorated in a range of well-fired enamel colours which are instantly recognizable when compared with the marked examples of their work and it is worth noting that there is far less flaking on them than occurs with later factories. In particular, in addition to the occasional passages of underglaze cobalt blue, the same cobalt oxide was used as an overglaze enamel in two distinct shades, a dark rich royal blue and a very pale sky blue. The green enamel was a sage shade and the yellow was not bright but a sort of subdued Cornish cream. In contrast the red was rich and deep and the odd touches of orange light-toned and cheerful. There, I told you it was difficult, but it might give you some idea. The exception to the sage green occurs when the base of some of them is decorated with those little clumps of clay threads which I call parsley since no one else seems to have invented a word for it. Always on Lloyd-Shelton figures this is coloured in two enamels, bright green with a touch of the clear orange in the centre. Thomas Parr used similar orange and green for his parsley but the clumps were bigger and the two colours never so carefully separated into orange centre and green edge.

Above all, John and Rebecca loved gilding, and whoever it was they employed in that department was very good indeed for some of the decorative use of fine quality gold is as superb as anything which came out of the grand factories like Minton or Spode, or indeed Derby or Rockingham if it comes to that. Isn't it strange that figures of such quality could have been produced in a factory about which we know virtually nothing except the name, and we wouldn't even have known that if they hadn't

152. *"Turn about an' wheel about an' do jis so, An' ebery time I turn about I jump Jim Crow."* The American negro impersonator Thomas Dartmouth Rice at the Surrey Theatre, London in 1836. Impressed Lloyd Shelton. *c.*1836. 6¼ ins.

153. Napoleon I. Both versions are by Lloyd, that on the right having a more complicated mould and much richer gilding. It is evidence that the factory production was extensive enough to cater for different markets. *c.*1840. 8¾ ins.

occasionally marked some of their figures. (152)

Apart from the gilt decorative patterns which they used on the body of the figures for waistcoats and women's dresses and so on, their most distinctive use of gilding was the generosity with which it was applied. (153, 155–157) The underbrims of hats, lapels on jackets, and the band of gold which was often used to set off the base was much broader than similar gilding on other contemporary figures. The Colour Plate 3 in my book *The Victorian Staffordshire Figure* shows three Lloyd Shelton figures which illustrate this very clearly and also gives a good idea of the very individual use of their parsley decoration.

While I'm at it I would now like to correct the caption to that colour plate where I tentatively ascribed the middle figure as possibly representing Gentleman John Jackson, the champion prize fighter. I have subsequently found that the Lloyds were working from a print of The Woodman, a painting by Thomas Barker of Bath. The print was well known and popular in the potteries having been engraved by Bartolozzi as early as 1792 and the figure is a very accurate version of it down to the smallest details.

The Lloyds, like their successors later in the Victorian period, obviously used prints as sources for some of their figures. The Woodman is a good example and they must have been one of the very first factories to see and copy the prints of James Thom's sculptures of Tam o'Shanter and Souter Johnny, the famous characters in Robert

154. An unrecorded portrait figure of Grace Darling unmarked but showing many characteristics of the Lloyd factory in Shelton. *c.*1840. 5 ins.

155. Fine gilding on the base of this large poodle by John and Rebecca Lloyd. *c.*1835. 8 ins.

Burns' poem. Thom finished the sculptures about 1830 and they were so successful that they were exhibited in several parts of the country before they became part of a permanent monument to Burns at Ayr in Scotland. The figures remained popular for years and many later versions were made in Staffordshire but none of them approach the Lloyd figures for delicacy and quality. I haven't succeeded in finding the original print source for the delightful little portrait of Grace Darling (154) but there must have been hundreds of them published when she made her dramatic rescue of the crew of the wrecked steamer *Forfarshire*. Her father was the lighthouse keeper on the lonely Farne Islands off the stormy coast of Northumberland and was unable, through illness, to row the tiny rescue boat, so our heroine Grace rowed it herself as the figure clearly suggests. Incredibly the delicate oar has survived intact and this is the only known example of this portrait which must have been made either to celebrate the rescue itself in 1838, or as a memorial to her early death from consumption in 1842.

It is probable that Grace Darling was a Lloyd figure, it has all the quality and fine workmanship but not much gold. If it was a memorial piece perhaps they felt it would have been too cheerful with heavy gilding. Certainly the sage green of her dress is typical of Lloyd and the concave underside of the base shows "wipe" marks as though the potter had wiped it with a cloth before glazing, a feature I have sometimes noted on marked Lloyd pieces. If the Lloyds were for once going easy on the gilding then I can only say that they were displaying an uncharacteristic sense of propriety, for in many of their figures they simply couldn't resist it. Even the little Italian boy bird seller (150) who in real life would have been decidedly grubby if not ragged, was given a couple of gold fleurs-de-lis on the knees of his trousers. I have seen two versions of this figure, one all white and gold was marked Lloyd-Shelton and this multi-coloured version with his sage green coat and royal blue cap is impressed underneath the base THE ITALION [sic] BOY. The poor little bird is, needless to say, in a gilded cage.

But the most wildly over-gilded Lloyd figures must surely be those shown in Figure 157. Again they are taken from prints by Thomas Barker of The Woodman and a companion. (158) The Barker originals are suitably dressed in rough patched labourers' clothes, but by the time the Lloyds had finished with them they look more like Prince Charming and Dandini. Never mind, it shows willing and does at least give them a kind of dotty and ridiculous charm. At least the source was English; the Lloyds never fell into the worst excesses perpetrated in some of the Minton figures.

Something quite awful happened to the figures made in the Minton factory in Staffordshire. They started off sanely enough and there are some very good early glazed and coloured porcelain portraits, notably a fine standing figure of a young Lord Byron about 6 inches high on a simple oblong base. Later they became obsessed with elaborate rococo bases and the ultimate horror of lace embellishments appeared. I'm not making this up, I promise you. Real lace was dipped into liquid clay and fired into its ghastly simulacrum in porcelain. Thankfully, most of it has not survived the

117

156. Theatre or opera, it has been listed as Mr Wood as Atabarnes in *Artazerxes* but I have not seen the print. A fine figure typical of the factory. Impressed mark Lloyd Shelton is known on other identical examples. *c.*1835. 14 ins.

157. The most elaborate use of gilding I have found on Lloyd figures. Their version of Thomas Barker's fierce lurcher dog isn't quite right, either. The trimming knife can be seen in the woodman's belt, the pipe and the axe were too vulnerable to make in porcelain and were often added later carved in wood, or fashioned in metal. *c.*1845. 10, 10½ ins.

158. The Woodman. The Bartolozzi engraving after the painting by Thomas Barker of Bath which the Lloyds used as their source for the woodman in Figure 157.

handling of time but it was a sad example of a fine English factory seduced into an alien fashion best forgotten if not forgiven. Minton figures are strongly reminiscent of continental factories and were intended to be. They are quite untypical of the splendid mainstream of native genius which poured out of the wretchedly poor pot-banks in every overcrowded township of the Staffordshire Potteries. Minton's influence on these vigorous and original contemporaries was mercifully minimal. They saw Minton's figures and remained true to their own inspiration. I have seen a pottery copy by Thomas Parr of a Minton figure of "Arabia" (159) but then Parr's figures are not typical of Staffordshire either and always leaned towards a porcelain style. While I think of it, there is a new fact about Thomas Parr's figures which has not been recorded before. All previous reference books have said that Parr always used overglaze enamel colours and never the distinctive underglaze cobalt blue. However, during the last ten years I have had several figures which were unquestionably by Thomas Parr but which also had large areas of cobalt blue. So it is more accurate to say that he used it less than his contemporaries, but that he definitely did use it.

Later on, Minton came to its senses and made some splendid figures in both bisque and the new parian porcelain. It's a matter of taste, of course, but any one who loves the essential Englishness of Staffordshire figures can hardly be expected to appreciate the simpering vacuity of Minton's nineteenth century females forever staring into space

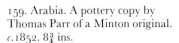

159. Arabia. A pottery copy by
Thomas Parr of a Minton original.
c.1852. 8¾ ins.

160. Mark on the back of the base of the Dickens'
characters in *Nicholas Nickleby*.

like bored, overdressed whores in a Dresden brothel. At least Staffordshire portraits are
forthright and honest, both Queen Victoria and Maria Manning who shot her lover
and buried him in her kitchen are not afraid to look us straight in the eye.

Minton should have been an obvious candidate for some of our early unmarked
porcelain portraits, but Godden's painstaking and definitive book on the factory and its
products makes it plain in the published list of figures that whoever made them it
wasn't Minton. It's doubly disappointing in that both the Derby modellers Edward
and his brother Samuel Keys were working at the factory from at least 1830 and
possibly earlier, but their influence in the Minton list was hardly noticeable. Edward
left to work on his own in 1842 but there is no record of anything he produced then and
he must have finally abandoned all hope of commenting on the real world around him
when he joined Wedgwoods in 1845. Samuel is said to have worked for several firms
until he joined Minton possibly at the same time as his brother. Both of them were fine
modellers and the quality, style and taste of the figures they both made at Derby would
suggest that they could have been responsible for some of our early portraits either
working for themselves or for unknown employers.

161. There are six figures in the complete set, the other two being Smike and Wackford Squeers. *c.*1839. 8¼, 8, 8½, 8½ ins.

162. Transfer printed marks.

There were many other potters working in Staffordshire in that first quarter of the nineteenth century who were capable of producing porcelain figures of the same high quality as the Lloyds, but without at least one marked example as a touchstone it must remain largely a matter for speculation.

The Ridgways were a famous family of Staffordshire potters established at Shelton from about 1792. One member of the family, William Ridgway, produced quality earthenwares at the Bell Works in Shelton and at the Church Works in nearby Hanley. The Bell Works changed hands in 1854. William appears to have been in business with his son but there is an entry in the Hanley Rate Records of 1837–1839 which records a partnership between William Ridgway and Ralph Mayer Robey. This fact would be of but passing interest had not a set of porcelain figures come to light all bearing their

163. James Braidwood. The crudeness of the title might be an indication of the haste with which the portrait was produced. The little fireman on the right is about the same date. *c.*1861. 14¾, 5⅛ ins.

mark. A mark conveying such explicit and precise information as to gladden the heart of any researcher. (160)

All the figures are superbly potted and are all titled with the names of the principal characters in Dickens' novel *Nicholas Nickleby*. Until quite recently only three of these figures had been recorded, Ralph Nickleby, Kate Nickleby and Wackford Squeers, to which I have been able to add Mrs. Nickleby, Smike and finally Nicholas himself. Each of these splendid portraits bears on the back of the base the following printed inscription: "Published June 15th 1839 by Ridgway and Robey. Hanley. Staffordshire Potteries." Not bad is it? A mark really couldn't be much more explicit than that, and yet, infuriatingly, it raises more questions than it answers.

Why are these the only six known examples of figures to bear this mark which is presented to us so unequivocally – with pride even. If the partnership lasted for a very short time that might account for it, in which case it is possible that Ridgway went on alone in his factories to produce unmarked figures of a similar quality. (161, 162)

The date of the figures – June 15th, 1839 – is interesting. In publishing *Nicholas Nickleby*, Dickens followed the same method that he had already used with great success when *Pickwick Papers* was issued in twenty monthly instalments between April 1836 to November 1837. He began to write the first instalment of *Nicholas Nickleby* on February 7th, 1838, his twenty-sixth birthday, and it was not completed until September 1839.

164. "Nicholas hints at the probability of his leaving the company." Original illustration by Phiz, 1838.

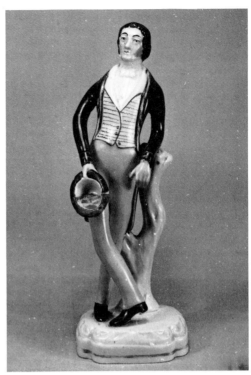

165. A contemporary copy of Ridgway and Robey's Nicholas Nickleby. *c.*1840. 8 ins.

166. Sam Weller and Mr Pickwick. Possibly Ridgway and Robey. *c.*1837. 7½ ins.

167. "First appearance of Mr Samuel Weller." Original illustration by Phiz. *c.*1836.

So that means Ridgway and Robey had launched their figures on to the market before the novel was finished. It is a remarkable example of how commercially minded the Staffordshire potters could be and the speed with which they could work when public interest was at its height and their figures were likely to be in greatest demand.

It might be said that "published" here merely indicated the date when the copyright was established, but the common commercial sense of the Staffordshire potters argues strongly against this; when they moved, they moved quickly. When James Braidwood, the London fire chief, was killed in the great fire of Tooley Street in June 1861, the potters made a titled portrait figure of him in uniform and had it on sale in the streets at his funeral a week later. (163)

All the original illustrations in the monthly instalments of *Nicholas Nickleby* were drawn by Phiz, the pseudonym of H. K. Browne. When the three figures of Ralph and Kate Nickleby and Wackford Squeers were first noted the original source on which they were modelled was not immediately apparent. With the discovery of Mrs Nickleby, Smike and Nicholas it can be seen quite clearly that the set of six figures were taken from the original Phiz drawings. Nicholas and Smike are almost exact ceramic copies of the drawings and the others follow very closely indeed. (164)

When I checked the original edition of *Pickwick Papers* I was able to identify the porcelain portraits (166) and to see that they too had been based exactly on the Phiz illustration of Sam Weller and Mr Pickwick himself (167). Although the figures are untitled and unmarked and the colours used are quite different from the Nickleby set, they are of a similar quality and not dissimilar in style. It's possible that they were an early production of Ridgway and Robey and if not, then just one more example of an unknown Staffordshire factory equalling Derby and Rockingham for quality.

It's very odd that our potters were not more influenced by Dickens and his illustrators. His views and sympathies coincided so closely with their own that I would have expected them to have made many more figures of his characters and certainly a bust or a portrait of Dickens himself. There is a later flat-back group of Sairey Gamp and Betsey Prig based on a Phiz illustration in *Martin Chuzzlewit* and I have seen a few contemporary copies of the Nicholas Nickleby figure (165) but really that's about all one can claim with certainty. This is not to say that more Dickens characters will not turn up, and even though I have looked closely at all the original illustrations I always have an uneasy feeling that I have missed some. Where Phiz was used as a source the potters were frequently selective, isolating their characters from a print which was sometimes crowded with people and incident. It would be easy to miss one.

While it's a shame that so few of the Ridgway and Robey figures were made, it shows the skill available in Staffordshire and that apart from John and Rebecca Lloyd there were others capable of producing fine quality porcelain portrait figures to rival those of Derby and Rockingham.

Who else? Well, John and Richard Riley had a prosperous partnership in Burslem

168. Princess Charlotte. Marked bust by John and Richard Riley of Burslem. *c*.1817. 17⅛ ins.

and were active from 1802 to about 1828, first in a small factory in Nile Street and later at the Hill Street Works from 1815. They both seem to have died very suddenly in early middle age and their business was announced for sale in *The Staffordshire Advertiser* on January 29th, 1831 and again in April. The sale was to be on the premises of the Hill Street Works and everything had to go without reserve including all the existing stock. This last is interesting because the advertisements specifically mention figures and chimney ornaments together with the blocks and working moulds from which they were made.

Now I have not seen a figure marked from the factory but we did find a very fine quality porcelain bust of Princess Charlotte (168) which was almost certainly made to commemorate her untimely death in 1817, and under the base it is marked J and R Riley. The bust is quite large, about 17 inches high so perhaps their mark was reserved for big pieces. If their figures and chimney ornaments were anything like this standard, and there is no reason to suppose they were not, then John and Richard Riley like the Lloyds of Shelton, and Ridgway and Robey, could well have made some of our figures. And who bought their original blocks and working moulds? Almost certainly another working potter. The frequency with which this happened in the Potteries helps to explain the great difficulties in attributing figures to a definite potter.

That's quite enough about who may or may not have made them. Let us be thankful that so many of them still exist and sell today for a tiny fraction of the price collectors will pay for Rockingham or Derby. As an example of their quality what shall we look at? What about Mr Van Amburgh and his wild animals, we couldn't choose a better figure to illustrate the very best of these early Lloyd Shelton portraits. (Colour Plate IV) It's quite true that he was an American lion tamer and was born in Kentucky, but for our purposes he was as much a part of our English scene as the young Queen herself. "The Brute Tamer of Pompeii" was known and instantly recognized not only in London but, through his provincial tours, all over England. He first arrived in 1838 and took London by storm.

At that time the theatre in England was in a sad state. Shakespeare, and indeed all legitimate drama, could only be legally presented at the two great patent houses of Covent Garden and Drury Lane. Not that their monopoly did them much good for it was a sad time for actors too. Macready was no Garrick and Charles Kean a poor substitute for his father Edmund. Both theatres failed financially with depressing regularity.

Mr Van Amburgh was no actor either, but he was most certainly a star, combining as he did the qualities of Tarzan, Errol Flynn and Evel Knievel. Like Tarzan he had a supporting cast of the fiercest lions, tigers, panthers and leopards, like Flynn he was very handsome, and like Knievel there was always the chance that you might see him killed. He was above all a superb showman.

Mr Bunn, the manager of Drury Lane, knew a winner when he saw one. His current production of Rossini's opera *La Gazza Ladra* was losing almost £100 a night, a huge sum in those days. He added Van Amburgh and his "celebrated felines" to the bill in a hippodramatic spectacular entitled *Charlemagne, or the Moors of Spain* and his box office receipts shot up by well over £100 a night. The highbrow critics wailed in dismay, of course, but it made no difference, Van Amburgh and his cats were a roaring success.

To those early Victorian theatre audiences, and certainly to the Queen herself, it must have come as a blessed relief after an earnest and desperately dull evening of Macready at Covent Garden in Lord Byron's turgid drama *Werner*. True she had managed a wan smile for Mr Macready and remembered her royal training long enough to say, "I am very much obliged to you".

Her duty done she promptly visited the rival establishment at Drury Lane three times in one fortnight to watch Mr Van Amburgh, with his beautiful whiskers and lovely bare legs, marvellously accoutred as a Roman Gladiator: "The Brute Tamer of

126

169. Isaac Van Amburgh's curtain call at Drury Lane. *c.*1838. 6¼ ins.

170. The source for the Lloyd group of Van Amburgh's act. A print on a marked souvenir mug by John and Robert Godwin of Cobridge Staffordshire. *c.*1838. 3½ ins.

Pompeii" in all his glory. She watched enthralled as he wrestled fearlessly with his snarling, spitting jungle cats, performing such feats of skill and daring with them as she had never imagined in her quiet palace at Kensington. His fiercest lion, whose earsplitting roars had trembled the very diamonds in her tiara, was made – could one believe it? – to fulfil the Biblical prophesy and to lie down meekly with a lamb. (76)

There is something rather touching about the enthusiasm and happiness of this nineteen-year-old girl as she watched and applauded the handsome lion tamer from Louisville. She was persuaded with no difficulty at all to inspect the animals on the stage itself after one of the performances and to watch Mr Van Amburgh feed them. (Macready could scarcely believe his ears and said so in his diary.) The visit was a great success. The lion which had dutifully resisted the lamb now promptly fought with the panther for the last chunk of meat so ferociously that the bars of the cage seemed about to burst open and deposit the snarling catherine wheel of fur, tails and teeth at the feet of the Monarch. One of the ladies-in-waiting seriously considered fainting until she caught the Queen's eye and thought better of it. Victoria was enchanted with it all. "The dear creatures," she was heard to murmur when the pandemonium had subsided, and she departed reluctantly to rule the Empire.

Now unlike the Grace Darling, the Van Amburgh figure has so many exact features in common with pieces marked Lloyd-Shelton as to make it certain beyond all reasonable doubt that it was a product of the same factory. The ingenious modelling in the round is typical as is the body of heavy white porcelain. All the enamel colours in their distinct subtleties of shade are there and the very individual brushstroke painting of the hair and eyes. But most characteristic of all is the generous Lloyd gilding, including the identical fleurs-de-lis found on the knees of the little Italian bird seller.

Like the other Lloyd portraits the Van Amburgh group was based on a print. It was most likely commissioned by him for it shows the same scene, the identical costume in every detail and has the leopard crouching on his shoulders. Think of those claws! Even my ginger tom cat is agony when he decides to sit on my shoulder while I'm writing. While we're at it you might just as well have a look at the back view too. I think it's almost as enchanting as the front and see how cleverly Lloyd has dispensed with the short supporting column using the back of the lioness instead. Not bad is it? Do admit. (169)

I think Van Amburgh might have commissioned the print himself because it was transfer printed on to cheap pottery mugs made by John and Robert Godwin of Cobridge in Staffordshire. (170) They were made to be sold as souvenirs when Van Amburgh travelled all over England and must have had his approval at least. Anyway John and Rebecca Lloyd certainly saw this print and used it as the source of their group. I have no record of it having been sold like the mugs, it would have been comparatively expensive for a souvenir. On the other hand, it was an obvious outlet for the figure and, as we have seen, Van Amburgh's appeal was not solely confined to the poor labouring classes.

Even though their style and material was different the Lloyds, like Sherratt before them and the later Victorians who followed them, were the true chroniclers of the lives of ordinary people in England. Their world was the pub and the travelling menagerie in a land where lovers were sailors and village girls not Venus kneeling in a shell with Cupid. They may have been a bit heavy handed with the gilding on some of their figures but at least they knew where they lived. There is no doubt that John and Rebecca Lloyd, together with some of their unrecorded contemporaries, made some of the finest and most neglected figures ever to come out of Staffordshire.

7
A Design for Murder
and Mayhem

Sherratt and Walton effectively slammed the door on the Neo-Classical tradition in the field of popular ceramics. In comparison the Woods and their imitators were insipid. Technically brilliant as they were, they lacked guts.

The guts and the blood and thunder, once they were established by the new schools in the early nineteenth century, remained true to the English tradition all through the century. This is the fact as far as the grass-root naïve potters were concerned, grander commercial factories like Mintons employed artists and modellers from all over Europe; the art director, Leon Arnoux, was himself French.

This wasn't, of course, solely a nineteenth century innovation; Chelsea, Derby and Bow had all earlier copied from continental factories and even their treatment of essentially English themes and subjects is largely overlaid with the formality of German Principalities and the artificial taste of the French aristocracy. It was the nineteenth century potters of Staffordshire who were the first to challenge this continental influence on a commercial scale and who were to produce figures in both pottery and porcelain which were completely English in both concept and execution. There were lapses, and occasionally a potter like Thomas Parr of Burslem made some figures which he had copied directly from Minton. But such variants from the new English style were rare. The vast majority of small potteries in Staffordshire turned their backs upon all foreign influences and recorded their own world about them with an enthusiasm and gusto which is unique in the annals of ceramic art and it is only now beginning to be assessed and appreciated.

The importance of this nineteenth century revolution for present day collectors is very great indeed. It means that a huge new field has opened up for them, full of excitement and possibilities. No new collector, unless he is very rich, can afford the early salt-glaze pieces or the schools of Astbury and Whieldon. The early nineteenth century Sherratt and Walton pieces are still to be found although they can command quite high prices for fine and rare examples. Real opportunities lie in recognizing those fine pieces described in the last chapter; the porcelain groups by John and Rebecca Lloyd of Shelton and other similar pieces by their unknown contemporaries.

Even greater opportunities are now being recognized in the period from 1840 onwards. According to Haggar, the Lloyds were potting up to about 1850 and their

171. Victoria with her first child, the Princess Royal, impressed Lloyd Shelton. *c.*1840. 6¾ ins.

172. Victoria and Albert. Her wedding gift to him was the Star and Badge of the Garter in diamonds and he wears it here. Lloyd Shelton. *c.*1840. 6¾ ins.

marked figures of their final decade show that they were slowly abandoning the complexity of their earlier productions and moving into a more simple style which was to merge into the mainstream of the naïve art we are more familiar with for the rest of the century. One of their few marked examples of this period is a pair of Albert and Victoria with the young Queen nursing her first born child, the baby Princess Royal, born in 1840. In style they are not so very different from many other early Royal portraits, and although they are carefully modelled and of good quality they are far less complicated than the figures the Lloyds had been producing in the earlier period 1820–38. (171)

It seems reasonable to assume that the reason for this later simplicity of style was economic. The early years of the new English style had ambled along without any great excitement. Sherratt had discovered the fascination of the fairgrounds and recorded Corder's murder in the Red Barn, the Lloyds paid tribute to the heroism of Grace Darling and were increasingly interested in the world of theatrical heroes and melodrama. The most theatrical heroine of them all, the young eighteen-year-old Queen, swept them all off their feet in 1837 and created such an increased demand for images of her and her family, and indeed for all things native and English, that simplicity of style became essential if the potters were to be able to exploit it to its full commercial potential.

173. Victoria and Albert in riding habit. Lloyd Shelton. *c.*1840. 8 ins.

174. Punch and Judy shows were popular throughout the nineteenth century. Fine quality porcelain. *c.*1845. 8¼, 8½ ins.

The Royal bonanza was a godsend to our Staffordshire potters and the Queen and her growing family must have laid the foundations of prosperity for many a tiny pot-bank which might otherwise have failed financially and been forced to stop production. The Royal family were faithfully recorded on every conceivable occasion, births, marriages, at play and on state appearances. What Victoria did was to confirm the English school in their conviction that they need never look to anywhere but England for their inspiration. Once they'd got the bit between their teeth they set to with grateful enthusiasm to record all things English with enormous industry and enthusiasm.

In an age without films, radio or television, and at a time when even newspapers were without illustrations until the first primitive woodcuts appeared, it was largely left to the potters of Staffordshire to fill the gap and supply their fellow countrymen with images of their pageantry, history and current affairs. What is more they were in three-dimensional full colour and as immediate to the customers who bought them as any television programme is to us today. Like television images they came right into the home and must have had almost as big an impact except, mercifully, they couldn't speak.

It is really quite remarkable that it has taken so long for this astonishingly vigorous school of English potters to be appreciated by collectors. Even today with inflation rampant all around us there are wonderful opportunities for collectors of nineteenth century Staffordshire figures to add pieces to their collections which will inevitably gradually rise in price, and in some cases become beyond the reach of many, just as the earlier figures of the eighteenth century have done. So far, collectors in this field have understandably tended to concentrate on the named or identifiable portraits of the personalities of the day. I know collectors who have built up enviable groups of portrait figures reflecting the theatre, royalty, crime or the various military adventures throughout the period. There is, I believe, one aspect of collecting which has not yet been fully explored and which deserves more serious consideration.

No one knows who the designers or modellers were in these unrecorded, primitive pot-banks. In many cases it must have been the owner himself. Haggar writes of a man called George Hood, a potter who had been a successful manufacturer of earthenware toys in Tunstall but who had failed in his enterprise and had been reduced to the ownership of a miserably poor pot-bank in Burslem. In a fascinating autobiography called *When I was a Child* in which an old potter, C. Shaw, remembers working as a boy in Hood's little factory, there is a reference to Hood in his tiny stuffy room moulding little "toper-publicans". The inference is clear that many of those small pot-banks had no trained designer or modeller working for them. The gain is ours for the unforced natural designs they produced are so full of uninhibited joy and freedom of movement as to make the heart lift up with pleasure and delight. I notice with interest that over the last four or five years there is a small but growing group of discerning collectors who are concerned with design for its own sake, and not only in the portraits of famous personalities of the day.

It's always interesting for a dealer to notice the beginning of new trends in the tastes of his collectors and no one is better placed to observe them. After all, the dealer is the man who opens his door and is the first to learn what they are looking for.

Ten years ago I could have counted the number of serious American collectors on one hand. Now, more and more of them are becoming interested. Not so much in the rare portrait figures, that field is still largely the preserve of collectors in this country. What the Americans have discovered is the wonderful simplicity of the design in so many of the decorative figures. They love the bright, uninhibited freedom of both line and colour and are astute enough to realize that they can buy these original works of native art for a fraction of the price they would have to pay for a modern equivalent or indeed for an example of primitive African tribal art. How long the supply will keep pace with the demand, I don't know. Already I see signs that interior designers are entering the market and that must, in the nature of things, make it increasingly difficult for ordinary collectors to find the bargains which are so freely available today. Nevertheless, it always takes time for trends to get under way and thanks to the prolific industry of the Staffordshire potters in the nineteenth century there should be many opportunities for the discerning collector for some years to come.

175. Lane and Walker were made to commemorate the long-awaited prize-fight with Lane as challenger for the Lightweight title of All England. Walker was almost certainly bribed to lose. The resulting scandal and rage of his backers forced him to flee to America. These are the only figures of Lane and Walker known to have survived. Tom Cribb, once Heavyweight Champion of All England, died in poverty in the same year, 1848, and together with his opponent, the American Molyneaux, was issued as a companion pair to commemorate their bloody battle in 1811. All four c.1848. 7¼ ins.

Just look for a moment at some of these delightful examples of the true English potters' art owing nothing to outside influences. They are as bright and as happy as a chorus by Gilbert and Sullivan or a brass band on a sunny day. Naïve, primitive, yes they are that, and something more, for they have all the enthusiasm and simplicity of a child. It is a gift which most adults lose when childhood is only a distant memory. Only a few artists have retained the same innocence of expression in later life, Le Douanier Rousseau, Picasso, Stanley Spencer and today Hockney, all have that greatest gift of all, the gift of expressing simple enthusiasm without a wasted line or an unnecessary embellishment. And there in Staffordshire in the nineteenth century was a whole school of potters often poor, mostly illiterate, and for the most part anonymous, producing such a glorious outpouring of simple form and colour as to make us marvel that it has taken us so long to recognize it for what it is.

Once Victoria had alerted the potters to their true heritage the floodgates were open. Gradually they abandoned the complicated moulds necessary for the fine porcelain groups and figures of the Lloyds. The greater use of white Cornish clay gave them an earthenware body which lent itself extremely well to the more simple designs. The pageantry of Victoria's coronation was soon eclipsed by her rapid descent into domesticity and whilst it was very satisfying for the potters to record the births of the

176. Sir Robert and Lady Sale. *c*.1843. 7¼ ins.

royal children, there were limits to the number of permutations on a theme. From babies in swaddling clothes they were modelled in every conceivable situation, real or imagined. Guarded by angels, nursed by Victoria and Albert, seated on miniature thrones or perched precariously on ponies or pet goats they were best sellers; the potters knew it and were grateful, but they longed to exploit the new mood of patriotism. What they really needed was a war and unfortunately England was at peace. A brief respite came in 1838 with some unpleasantness in Afghanistan.

When eventually the British army under the command of Sir Robert Sale was beseiged in Kabul and forced to retreat, his wife, the indomitable Lady Sale, survived a hail of Afghan bullets ("fortunately I had only *one* ball in my arm"). She was made a prisoner for seven months and after a dramatic rescue by Sir Richmond Shakespeare launched into vivid print when her *Journal of the Disasters in Afghanistan* was published in 1843. She may not have had the publicity value of Queen Victoria but she was most certainly a heroine and the potters gratefully recorded her fame and that of her husband with a titled pair of equestrian figures issued that same year. There was sound commercial sense in topicality and the potters were not the only ones to cash in on it. On April 17th, 1843 the entire Afghan campaign was produced on the stage of the famous London Hippodrome theatre, Astley's Amphitheatre, just south of

Westminster Bridge. The cast included a multitude of horses, soldiers, mules and elephants as well as Sir Robert and Lady Sale, and it was a print of this production that the potters copied exactly for their figures of the heroic couple. (176)

Once the pattern for the new school of potters was established, Astley's was to be a mine of inspiration for them. The theatre had long specialized in *Gloires Militaires*. The Duke of Wellington himself had gone to see their version of *The Battle of Waterloo* in 1824 and it was to be a firm favourite with the public for many years after that. It undoubtedly accounts for the huge numbers of Napoleon figures of which the potters could never make enough to satisfy the demand; more Staffordshire portraits of the Emperor were made than even those of the Queen herself. While England remained obstinately at peace, the potters had to make do with the past triumphs of Nelson and Wellington and for the rest of the 1840s were reduced to recording life in England making portraits of Cobden and Peel, the heroes of the repeal of the Corn Laws in 1846, and rejoicing in the more notorious murders of the day with a complete coverage of the Rush crime and that of Maria Manning.

Since Staffordshire pottery is essentially about people, let us pause and indulge ourselves, just as did the good citizens who bought it, to experience the frisson of horror and fascination when Maria Manning stared down at them from their tasselled mantel-shelves in the gloomy winter of 1849.

Mr Manning, as we shall see, was not unconnected with the case but the single minded industry of his wife makes one think of her first. Born Marie de Roux in Switzerland and a former lady's maid to Lady Blantyre, she had before her marriage an affair with a Mr Patrick O'Connor, a man of modest but enviable wealth. It was, however, the more attractive physical endowments of Frederick Manning that won the lady's heart and hand and eventually they set up as proprietors of a beer-house in London's Hackney Road. (177)

Maria was now faced with that vexing puzzle of how to have your cake and eat it. After an uncharacteristic period of vacillation during which she returned to Patrick and the fleshpots only to be yanked back firmly and unceremoniously to the beer-house nest by Frederick, she allowed her ruffled feathers to settle and applied her best endeavours to the problem anew. Her solution had the merit of simplicity if not of originality and, having got it all quite clear in her own mind, she proceeded to brief her husband step by step.

The Mannings had by now moved to lodgings in Minver Place, Bermondsey, and it was here that, after certain necessary preparations had taken place, Mr and Mrs Manning extended the civilized hand of reconciliation and friendship and invited Mr O'Connor round for dinner on the August 19th, 1849.

The preparations were not solely concerned with the meal itself and indeed I can find no record in contemporary accounts of what Swiss delicacies Maria might have had in mind. Cynic that I am, I suspect she had none. No, the hospitality she had

177. Maria Manning and Frederick George Manning. *c.*1849. 9, 9½ ins.

178. There are at least fifteen different versions of this very popular pair. *c.*1850. 9¾ ins.

envisaged was not of a culinary nature.

On July 28th a large chisel the size of a crowbar and a quantity of quicklime had been delivered to Minver Place and on August 8th Mr Manning dutifully bought a shovel and dug a large hole in the kitchen floor. The following day Patrick O'Connor arrived promptly for dinner and was equally promptly shot through the head by Maria and finished off by Frederick with the crowbar. As he put it later to the police with commendable frankness, "I never liked him very much and I battered in his head with a ripping chisel".

With O'Connor buried and the kitchen flagstones neatly cemented back in place, Maria made several visits to his home removing jewellery, money and bonds. Unfortunately she seems not to have shared the financial expertise of many of her countrymen and the disposal of the bonds defeated her. She fled to Edinburgh leaving Frederick penniless and alone in Minver Place: almost alone anyway. He stuck it for two days – imagine it! – and then panicked, travelling to the Channel Islands.

O'Connor's family became suspicious and quite soon the Mannings' kitchen floor was dug up by the police. She was arrested in Edinburgh and he on the island of Jersey. Both blamed the other and neither would look at, nor speak to the other throughout the trial at the Old Bailey in October 1849. They were united if not reconciled on the scaffold erected on the roof of Horsemonger Lane Gaol, where Charles Dickens and a party of friends watched them hanged on November 13th having paid ten guineas for the tickets. Maria, tasteful to the last, wore black satin for the occasion which promptly went out of fashion, unlike public executions themselves which were to prove extremely popular for another twenty years.

The potters loved it all, murder wasn't as good as a war but having found their theme they gratefully recorded crimes like the Mannings' and that of James Rush of Potash farm, as we have already seen. 1849 was a very good year for murders but when the blood and thunder, thud and blunder, of contemporary murder was slack they turned to villains of earlier times and slapped them into clay with equal enthusiasm. It explains why so many splendid colourful equestrian pairs were made of the highwaymen Dick Turpin and his partner Tom King.

The many myths and legends which have grown up around these two "Gentlemen of the Road" date from the romanticized view of their characters contained in Harrison Ainsworth's novel *Rookwood* which was published in 1834 and produced as a hippodramatic spectacle in the arena of Astley's Amphitheatre many times thereafter.

Turpin and King flourished in the early eighteenth century. In real life Turpin was a thug, an ex-butcher who robbed and murdered without compunction, and King was no better. Turpin shot King by mistake when they were surprised by law officers. He himself survived until April 1739 when he was hanged at York for horse stealing. Ainsworth made glamorized heroes of them but it was all fiction, there never was that romantic ride to York on gallant Black Bess, no honour and less chivalry. The fact and the fiction may be judged by comparing two quotations. The first comes from the Astley's production of March 26th, 1841. Dick: (to old lady, a passenger in a stage coach) "Here, mother, take back thy purse and here's a gold guinea to go with the pence in it, for Dick never could, nor never shall, rob the old and the poor." The second comes from an account in the *London Evening Post* of February 6th, 1735 describing how Turpin's gang robbed the house of the widow Shelley at Loughton in Essex. They threatened to burn and murder her when she refused to tell them where she had hidden her money. Turpin's actual words were: "God damn your blood you old bitch, if you won't tell us I'll set your arse on the grate."

So there he is, our bonny hero, and the Staffordshire potters made a fortune out of him and his partner, King. (178)

The potters had their theme and their style, all they really needed now was a new generation of heroes. There were limits to the subjects they could find in crime, royalty and politicians and no one in England could have been more gratefully patriotic when at last war was declared against Russia in March 1854.

🎄 8 🎄
Sailor Heroes

G. M. Trevelyan in his famous history dismissed the Crimean War as a foolish expedition to the Black Sea engendered by boredom. In 1854 there was certainly a feeling abroad in England that it was time to flex the national muscles and whip some sense into the "blackhearted Tsar of all the Russias" and yet it is easier now than in Trevelyan's time to recognize the real threat of letting Russia gain a firm foothold in the Mediterranean, a policy she has transparently pursued whenever opportunity has arisen, right down to the present day. Whatever historians might say the potters at least had no doubt where right lay and proceeded to chronicle the war with an enthusiasm which was to produce a wonderfully colourful display of naïve patriotic art such as has never been seen anywhere in the world before or since.

In the eighteen months which followed, the royal children bowed out of the limelight while the Queen was paired with each of her allies, Napoleon III, The King of Sardinia and The Sultan of Turkey. Albert was grouped with Napoleon too, and there were countless figures of the naval and military commanders in the field in dozens of shapes and sizes. As if that were not enough they made models of the main Russian fortresses Malakoff, Sebastopol and The Redan and fell gratefully upon a new heroine called Florence Nightingale. (179–188)

Now the interesting thing which appears when surveying the potters' production for the Crimean period is the great number of naval figures which they made. Having exhausted the army commanders and admirals, the potters realized that their greatest sales could be achieved by celebrating the ordinary fighting man and while they certainly made many figures of soldiers, the true heroes in the eyes of their public were the sailors who had so often saved England in the past and carried with them a reputation such as the poor English soldiers had never been able to equal. It seems rather unfair when one thinks of the great conquests which had added to the Empire by the courage and prowess of England's armies in the field, and yet it was always the sailors who held first place in the affections of the people. Memories were long and from the defeat of the Spanish Armada in 1588, England had looked to her "Wooden Walls", the battleships of her navy, to protect and preserve her. (189) It was, therefore, perhaps understandable that the British Sailor who alone stood between this country and any threat of armed invasion by sea should have attained an almost mystical aura of heroic glamour. It was a position he was to hold unchallenged right up to the day when the sea was no longer our last bastion of defence, and the air force fighter pilot succeeded to the role of hero extraordinary in the Second World War.

179. Florence Nightingale and wounded
Crimean officer. *c*.1855. 9¾ ins.

181. Allies: Victoria and Victor Emmanuel II.
c.1855. 14 ins.

180. Crimean Fortress Malakoff. *c*.1854. 6¾ins.

182. Napoleon III, Victoria and Victor
Emmanuel II. *c.*1854. 12 ins.

183. Victoria and Napoleon III. *c.*1854. 11 ins.

184. A memorial figure of Lord
Raglan, Commander of the
British Army in the Crimea, by
Thomas Parr. Only two
examples are known. *c.*1855.
12 ins.

185. The source for Figure 184.
The Illustrated London News,
Saturday July 7th 1855.

186. General Sir George Brown and General Sir James Simpson. Crimean Commanders. Simpson succeeded Raglan at his death. Both *c.*1855. 13 ins.

187. Crimean Gunner with French Tricolour and Union Jack. *c.*1855. 11¾ ins.

188. Crimean battle scene. *c.*1855. 11 ins.

144

189. The British Tar returns with his prize money. The foaming mug of beer carries the
slogan "Success to our Wooden Walls". Walton. *c.*1810. 10¼ ins.

190. Lower deck sailor. *c.*1800. 7¾ ins.

Examples of ceramic naval heroes before the nineteenth century are almost exclusively confined to portraits of famous admirals. Very occasionally the odd representative of life on the lower deck turns up (190) but they are very rare. The Ralph Woods made a plaque of a sailor picking up a girl on shore leave. (191) The boy is dressed in a mixture of civilian and naval dress which would have been common in 1780, standard uniform for ratings not having been recommended by the Admiralty until 1856.

The plaque is nearly always referred to in sale-room catalogues as "Patricia and her Lover" and was indeed so titled in Falkner's book *The Wood Family of Burslem* first published in 1912. In fact, the Woods copied it from a mezzotint published in 1780 by R. Sayer and J. Bennett and the source is exact down to the smallest detail. The mezzotint is from a series titled "Jack on a Cruise" and sub-titled: "Avast, there! Back your mainsail". (192)

The plaque is not only interesting as being one of the rare eighteenth century examples of the potters' interest in the lower-deck seamen, but as an early prototype of them using an exact copy of a print as their inspiration. Prints themselves had for some years been transferred directly on to pottery and porcelain by means of paper transfer printing, in particular by Sadler and Green of Liverpool, but the Wood plaque, by converting the print into a clay facsimile, was a new technique which was to be used by most of the Staffordshire potters throughout the nineteenth century. That they did so

191. "Jack on a Cruise. Avast, there! Back your mainsail." Ralph Wood plaque. *c.*1780. 13¾ ins. By courtesy of Messrs Christie, Manson and Woods.

192. The mezzotint source for Figure 191 published 1780 by R. Sanger and J. Bennett.

was to prove a boon for researchers in that field for if an untitled figure can be matched with a titled print which was its original source it can, in a delightfully satisfying way, identify the figure without any doubt; a procedure I have described in some detail in *The Victorian Staffordshire Figure.*

Simply by looking at the illustrations of the Victorian figures reproduced here it is possible to see with what delight the potters realized the rich mine they had uncovered in celebrating the adventures and bravery, the humour and the essential decency, all qualities they unhesitatingly attributed to the common sailor, the Jolly Jack Tar of Old England. They need no text to explain them, they were meant to sit on a cottage mantel-shelf and speak for themselves and they do it superbly, which is why they were made and sold in the first place and why they are so collectable today.

Once a collector knows of the love affair – for it is just that – between the potters and their sailor heroes, he very often becomes hooked into collecting nothing else. I speak from experience, for long before I became a dealer I was a collector of naval figures. (Colour Plate V)

The first sailor figures to appear in any numbers were probably made by John Walton during the surge of patriotic fervour engendered by the Napoleonic wars. Stylistically they date from about 1810 and include an early version of the ever popular

193. Sailor's Departure and Return. Walton c.1810. 9½, 9 ins.

"Sailor's Return" and "Sailor's Farewell", a theme which was very close to the public for whom they were made. An important sailor Toby Jug is an adapted version of an eighteenth century model by the Woods. It can be dated accurately to 1815 for the potter has added the word "Trafalgar" in moulded relief on either side of the sea chest on which the sailor sits and for good measure a medallion of Nelson's flagship the *Victory* appears titled on the back of it. (193–195)

A few more sailor figures appear in these early years of the century including a delightful version of a sailor boy's farewell by John and Rebecca Lloyd in the 1830s. (196) Where the royal children did get a look in it was more often than not dressed as sailors, and not as officers either, but uncompromisingly clothed in the uniform of the lower deck, a fashion which was to remain popular for little boys right up to the First World War in 1914.

The real flood of figures came with the Crimean War and the ordinary sailor continued to be a firm favourite throughout the rest of the century. Sailors were chronicled in every situation. They took leave of their wives and girl friends who were often shown assuming the men's civilian occupations as fisherwomen or farmers. They came home triumphantly waving their money bags (sailors traditionally collected their meagre pay only at the end of a voyage). They are seen spending it in pubs, ignoring the advice enjoined upon them in the Bible, the subject of a superbly potted figure titled "A

195. Nelson's ship *Victory*.
Impressed and titled
plaque on the back of the
Trafalgar Toby,
Figure 194. Detail.

194. The Trafalgar Toby. No other
example is known. Wood factory. *c*.1815.
$11\frac{1}{2}$ ins.

Mother's Last Gift'', in which she is seen thrusting a bible upon her departing sailor son. (197) At sea they manned the guns, they fought and were killed or died of disease, or survived to dance a victorious hornpipe, until the potters could finally show them celebrating the great peace of 1856. The victory did little to dampen the potters' enthusiasm, and sailors who had fallen on hard times can be found begging on the roadside with model boats or small children to emphasize their plight. The luckier wounded and limbless end their days in the uniform of Greenwich Hospital Naval Pensioners dreaming of past glories in the service of a grateful country.

Any great popular feeling such as the glorification of the British sailor was bound to find expression in other media. The newspapers and magazines were beginning to have illustrations even though they were laboriously produced by woodcut engravings. In both, the cult of the sailor was much in evidence and the potters frequently used their illustrations and adapted them as ideas for their figures. Perhaps the greatest celebration of the nautical theme, apart from the potters themselves, was the popular theatre which had been growing in size and influence at a tremendous rate since the

196. Sailor's Farewell. John and Rebecca Lloyd of Shelton. c.1835. 4¾ ins.

198. Off to sea with the harvest safe. Union Jacks were difficult for children to paint and time consuming. They do appear sometimes but this quick decoration was often substituted. c.1854. 11 ins.

197. A Mother's Last Gift. c.1854. 10 ins.

199. "Come Lass weep not for Jack." c.1854. 9¼ ins.

201. Holder for a pocket watch. *c.*1856. 11⅛ ins.

200. Jack Ashore. *c.*1855. 7¼ ins.

202. Begging Sailors with model boats and hungry children elicited sympathy after the war. Later professional beggars cashed in on the idea and in the 1860s and 70s both boats and children could be hired by the day. This lad must be genuine as he was made *c.*1856. 16¼ ins.

203. A young sailor offering money to a Pensioner of the Royal Naval Hospital Greenwich. c.1855. 8⅛ ins.

205. The Jolly Jack Tar. There are many different versions of this most popular figure. c.1855. 13½ ins.

204. One of the first figures to appear at the start of the Crimean War. c.1854 11½ ins.

206. Wounded naval officers, three wooden legs. This is the only known example. *c*.1856. 7 ins.

207. For Queen and Country. *c*.1857. 7¾ ins.

153

turn of the century. In 1800 London only had nine theatres, by 1840 the number had risen to over sixty. A similar pattern could be seen all over the country as the workers were forced into towns by the late tide of the Industrial Revolution.

Shakespeare and the classical dreams of the eighteenth century were disliked by the new audiences as much as were the Neo-Classical pottery products of the Ralph Wood school. Like Sherratt and Walton, the new authors aimed to please a new proletarian audience and they found their inspiration in melodrama. A poor working man could readily identify with the problems of the new anti-hero in Buckstone's *Luke the Labourer* but for magic and excitement no modern hero could hope to compete with the Jolly Jack Tar and the nautical melodrama was established. It is true that the naval theme had been used earlier. Plays like *The Press Gang or True Blue* and *William and Susan or The Sailor's Sheet Anchor* were both produced in the eighteenth century, but with the larger audiences and the many new theatres the sailor hero became irresistible. With this new drama came new stars. Even the greatest names of the old classical school of acting were finding it difficult to please the public, and while Covent Garden and Drury Lane were falling on desperate days, the new popular theatres were packed to capacity to cheer their new naval heroes. Of these, the greatest of all was Thomas Potter Cooke.

Cooke made his debut at The Royalty Theatre in 1804 when he was eighteen, but he had already completed one career as a sailor in the Royal Navy which he had joined as a boy entrant sailing in the 18-gun brig HMS *Raven* under the command of Captain Prowse. He was present at the seige of Toulon and on February 14th 1797, aged eleven, he served under Admiral Jervis at the Battle of Cape St. Vincent when Commodore Nelson ignored fleet orders and was in large measure responsible for the complete defeat of the much larger Spanish fleet.

After further adventures, he narrowly escaped drowning by clinging to the rigging when the *Raven* was wrecked in a gale off Cuxhaven. He contracted rheumatic fever but recovered to sail in HMS *Prince of Wales* to the blockade of Brest, and retired from the navy in 1802 at the signing of the Peace of Amiens.

Many actors became famous for their portrayal of sailor heroes, Gallot, Munden, Reeve, Yates, Campbell and O. Smith among them, but not one of them engaged the heart and imagination of the public as "Tippy" Cooke did. Here was the real thing: the seaman's lurching walk, the open honest face of a man who had fought with Nelson and Jervis and who had learned to dance the double hornpipe on the decks of the Royal Navy itself.

From an early appearance as Nelson at Astley's Amphitheatre he moved from one nautical success to another for the rest of his long stage career: notably as Dick Fid in Fitzball's *Red Rover* and Long Tom Coffin in *The Pilot* by the same author, but in 1829 at the Royal Surrey Theatre on the South Bank of the Thames he found the play and the part with which he was to be linked for the rest of his life: William the gallant sailor hero in Douglas Jerrold's *Black-Ey'd Susan or All in the Downs*. In all he played the part

785 times in theatres all over England including appearances at Drury Lane and Covent Garden where he appeared for the last time at his farewell performance in 1860.

His portrait in naval uniform appeared by the thousands in prints and on music covers everywhere and the potters used them frequently to make figures of the new nautical hero. They were commercially cute enough not to title them as T. P. Cooke so that they could have been just as saleable to audiences who had seen one of his many imitators, although some of them are such good likenesses as to make the attribution quite certain. (208)

Cooke died on April 4th, 1864 at 37 Thurloe Square, London, at the age of seventy-eight. His death certificate says that the cause of death was "Decay of Nature". His influence put a stamp on his devoted public for many years after that and *Black Ey'd Susan* was played at the Adelphi with William Terriss as late as 1897. We can read the scripts of Cooke's most famous sailor roles and the contemporary accounts of his performances in them – Dickens called him a genius – but only through the skill of the Staffordshire potters can we glimpse for a moment what he really looked like in the flesh on the stage. He lived to enjoy enormous success, he could count admirals among his friends and he could fill Covent Garden, that same vast theatre which we know today, when Kemble and other great Shakespearean stars were failing miserably.

There is a postscript to this story of Thomas Potter Cooke which is an example of how the appreciation of Staffordshire portrait figures can spur research and throw new light on the heroes beloved by our potters.

Some years ago there came into the shop a man whose interests and enthusiasms so closely followed my own that I told him the story of Cooke much as I have told it here, knowing that he would be as fascinated as I was myself. It is one of the great perks of my job, or indeed of any antique dealer, to meet fellow enthusiasts and we can and do count ourselves lucky that it is so.

Captain K. J. Douglas-Morris, D.L., Royal Navy is one of the world's great authorities on naval medals and if you think that medals in museums are a bit stuffy and dull then go, I beg you, to the gallery which bears his name in the Royal Naval Museum Portsmouth and discover just how wrong you were. His collection of naval medals there is quite simply one of the most original and exciting concepts of museum display to be seen anywhere in the world.

What Captain Douglas-Morris and his curator friend, Colin White, have done is to sweep away all previous ideas of presentation so that the gallery is not simply full of medals but alive with the presence of the men who won them. It was on this section of the museum that he came to seek our advice at Oliver-Sutton in the days when he was forming its collection of Staffordshire naval figures, so that it was inevitable that he should have been fascinated by Cooke's connection with the Royal Navy. One of the prints I showed him from my files had always been thought to represent Cooke in his

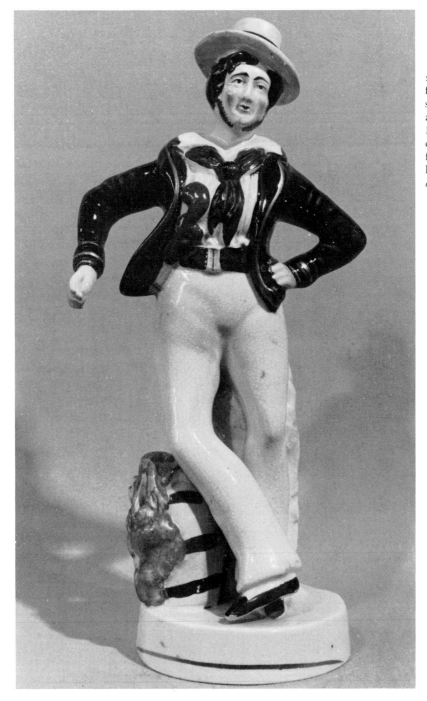

208. The most
famous stage
sailor of them
all. Thomas
Potter Cooke
dancing his
famous
hornpipe.
*c.*1825. 10½ ins.

156

209. T. P. Cooke and the medal. *c.*1849.

210. The Naval General Service Medal with the clasp of St. Vincent, awarded to Thomas Potter Cooke. *c.*1847. By courtesy of Captain K. J. Douglas-Morris, D.L.R.N.

157

most famous role as William in *Black-Ey'd Susan*. Judging by the uniform and by his appearance it is a likeness of him as he was towards the end of his career. It is even possible that it was based on a photograph, early examples of which are known to exist from the 1840s. Now of all the other prints I have of Cooke in his many roles as sailor-hero, this is the sole example which shows him wearing a medal of any sort. (209)

I had always thought that the medal would merely have been a stage prop, an extra touch of glamour for a stage hero. Douglas-Morris thought differently. He had listened carefully to my account of Cooke's naval career as a youth and on his next visit he was able to give me some interesting information. The Naval General Service Medal, he explained, was instituted in 1847 to cover 237 selected naval actions from 1793–1840. Cooke would certainly have been entitled to claim it and to wear it with the appropriate clasp of St. Vincent for that famous action in 1797. It was then that he told me the result of his researches.

He found that Cooke had indeed applied for and been awarded his Naval General Service Medal with the clasp of St. Vincent in 1847. Allow perhaps two years before he received the medal – that seems to have been the usual time to elapse before the actual medals were delivered – and what we may well see in the print is Cooke proudly wearing his decoration with the clasp of St. Vincent some day in 1849. Knowing now how he came to be eligible for it I doubt if he would ever have demeaned the honour by incorporating it in a fictional role. Long Tom Coffin, Dick Fid and William did not serve with Nelson at St. Vincent, but Thomas Potter Cooke did.

The story is not quite ended. After the account of his discoveries Captain Douglas-Morris asked if I knew what the Naval General Service Medal looked like and when I said no he produced a specimen from his collection for me to see.

"It has the clasp of St. Vincent," he said.

"So Tippy Cooke's medal would have looked exactly like this one?"

"Look at it carefully," he told me.

And there on the edge of the medal was engraved the name of the sailor to whom it had originally been awarded, T. P. Cooke. (210)

It seems a very satisfying way to end a chapter on nineteenth century naval heroes, but it does more than that. It illustrates very neatly how much more interesting it can be to collect Staffordshire figures than the pursuit of pretty porcelain ladies posing as the spirit of Arabia in lace knickers.

⚜ 9 ⚜
Summing Up

All collectors are lucky, obsessed as we are with a gentle mania to surround ourselves with the objects we love and admire. Perhaps those of us who collect Staffordshire pottery figures are luckier than most. What we bring together and put on our shelves is not simply an assembly of inanimate clay figures. However brightly coloured and attractive they may be in themselves they are the key to the door of another world. Not a world far back in the guesswork of history but only a stretched armslength away. They are the faithful chronicle of the wonders and horrors of their age, from the slow challenge of tradition at the end of the eighteenth century to the explosion of steam and ideas in the years of Victoria.

What makes us collectors? For myself I can trace my first interest back for over fifty years. Fifty-two, to be exact, when I was a very small boy. I was born in Wales in a village called Abersychan and it was there that I first saw a small collection of Victorian Staffordshire figures. Not in an antique shop, for the village did not possess anything so grand, but exactly where they were first intended to be seen, in a thoroughly satisfactory row on a cottage mantel-shelf.

In No. 5 Gas Square lived my Aunt Liza. She was in fact my great-aunt, my grandfather's sister. I loved her with the fierce affection of the very young and from time to time when my parents were away on holiday it was with Aunt Liza that I was sent to stay. It was no hardship.

There was a garden gate on which she used to let me swing, and then perhaps only some twelve feet would take me to her front door, a door with a thumb-latch which led like a theatre curtain rising directly into the living room.

For me, no Christmas card cottage could ever challenge the magic of that room. It is easy to over-romanticize one's early loves but my memory of Aunt Liza's cottage is needle sharp right down to the pattern of the wallpaper and the shape of her coalscuttle. Perhaps winter was the best time when the soft oil lamps and the firelight lit up her smile and jumped in her spectacles. She cooked her food on the blackleaded range before which on the stone flags was a rag rug and a ginger cat. Framing this scene was the mantel-shelf fringed in red plush with bobbles, the perfect stage setting for the little row of Staffordshire figures. They were everything to delight the eye of a child, simply moulded and a riot of colour, not to mention the subjects, soldiers, sailors, saints and sinners even murderers – like a miniature Madame Tussauds or the brightly lit stage of a theatre.

I will not pretend that I can remember every single one of those figures clearly,

211. England and Scotland. Crimean War, Superb simplicity of design and colour, like a brass band on a sunny day. *c.*1855. 9, 9⅛ ins.

although in my mind's eye now I can half persuade myself that the mantel was crammed with great rarities. Well perhaps it was, some I can still recall, a man in a top hat on a proud horse, a circus lady with multi-coloured drawers placed, rather daringly we thought, next to the American evangelists Moody and Sankey and the Reverend John Elias. Aunt Liza was not what my mother called Narrow Welsh. She looked very like Dame Edith Evans and her laugh, which I can still hear, was splendidly wicked, like a tonic.

In spite of the slight disparity in age – I was six and she was perhaps fifty – we would sit and talk the winter evenings away, and the right and proper topics for a child, too. The murder up the valley that had never been solved, "Although they do say . . .". The travelling menagerie and the fairground theatre that used to come to the field behind Gas Square when she was a girl. *Maria Marten and the Red Barn*, of course. And religion; yes, we talked a good deal of religion, she was a staunch Congregationalist and I was a Primitive Methodist so the rival merits needed to be discussed. The Prim's choir, she would concede, might just have the edge but it had to be admitted that when the Cong's minister preached of Hellfire, Aunt Liza and I used to hold hands tightly in the pew. (216)

212. The Indian Mutiny of 1857 produced figures of Generals Sir Colin Campbell and Sir Henry Havelock. *c*.1857. 11 ins.

It was Aunt Liza who took me to see my first silent picture, and one foggy Saturday afternoon in November to Pitt's Theatre in Pontypool to see Tod Slaughter in *Sweeney Todd the Demon Barber of Fleet Street*. Yes, winter was best. With luck I might catch a cold and be given her favourite remedy – and mine, a large mug of her elderberry wine warmed up in an enamel saucepan on the fire. Then to bed, and I was allowed to take the ginger cat with me for extra comfort. I can remember climbing up the ladder-steep stairs with my arms clasped round his long suffering furry belly and his four paws sticking out in front ready braced for the shock when I missed a step (I was quite sloshed of course) and then the feather bed with a brick in it hot from the oven and wrapped in Welsh flannel. It was to be expected, I suppose, that those early loves would stay with me through the years, the singing of the chapels, the theatre, wine, Staffordshire figures and cats.

As I grew up in the '20s and '30s she by some miracle – perhaps the elderberry wine – stayed exactly the same, she had a cure for everything, even old age. And No. 5 Gas Square stayed the same too, even the Staffordshire figures on the mantel. She remained loyal in her love of them and in this I was lucky for they had long since fallen from fashion, many of them swept away in the great reaction against Victorian taste in the

213. The only recorded figure of Saint Francis de Sales. It was possibly a special commission and made by Thomas Parr and is titled. *c.*1848. 14¾ ins.

214. Many figures were made of the Duke of Wellington but this one is unrecorded and may be unique. *c.*1852. 10¾ ins.

215. The American evangelists Dwight Lyman Moody and Ira David Sankey with friend. *c.*1873. 17 ins.

216. The Rev. Christmas Evans and the Rev. John Elias, Welsh non-conformist preachers. Elias taught in the first Sunday school in Caernarvonshire and Evans lost an eye in a religious brawl. Aunt Liza loved them. c.1856. $13\frac{1}{2}$, 14 ins.

early years of this century. But for her I might never have seen them and surely never in such a perfect setting. My parents and their generation disliked them intensely and the more they decried them the more I – perverse as all children with parents – defended and loved them.

The the war came and I joined the R.A.F. After six years I was demobilized and came home. To have been able to read that sentence in 1940 would have been pleasant.

Aunt Liza was definitely younger than ever. She was disappointed that I wasn't going to be a Methodist minister but I felt that one or two rather good sermons delivered by a drunken child of six to a congregation of two did not strictly constitute a true vocation and I became an actor instead.

I never forgot those brightly coloured Staffordshire figures from the happy memory of my childhood and I began to collect them for myself. They became first a gentle pleasure, then a hobby, and finally an obsession all the more absorbing when I found that very little was known about them and that if I was to learn more of their history I must discover it for myself.

In those days, plays often toured all over England sometimes for as long as sixteen weeks before coming into London, and I bought Staffordshire figures whenever I could find something of quality or interest. If I was lucky and the play settled into a long run

163

217. Welsh
Farmer and
Wife at market.
c.1848. 9½ ins.

218. The source for
Figure 217. By
courtesy of the
National Museum
of Wales. Welsh
Folk Museum
St. Fagans,
Cardiff.

164

219. Crossing the Brook.
Thomas Parr. *c*.1850. 9½ ins.

220. *Crossing the Brook*, detail from the painting by William Mulready R.A. exhibited Royal Academy, 1842. By courtesy of The Trustees of the Tate Gallery, London.

in London then I would spend all my days in the museums trying to identify and tabulate the spoils of the tour. It was a most happy and satisfying pursuit having all the elements of a good detective story and the most tantalizing of crossword puzzles. (217–223)

Sometimes, I'm afraid my interests were in some conflict. I spent the afternoon of Tuesday May 14th, 1946 content and happy in the library of the Victoria and Albert Museum. The rest of the cast of *French Without Tears* at the Vaudeville Theatre was less happy and content because I had quite forgotten that Tuesday was matinée day. I was forgiven, mainly I suspect from relief, because my understudy hadn't troubled to learn the part and scarcely remembered a line.

The research was, I now see, a refuge from the rat race of the theatre and the stress of the film and television studios. I was very happy and indeed lucky as an actor but the time would come when I should have to choose between the two main interests in my life. Some twenty or more years were to pass before I made that decision and then to be

221. Happy as a King. *c.*1869. 7½ ins.

222. Detail from the print of the painting, *Happy as a King* by William Collins R.A. The painting was first exhibited at the Royal Acadamy in 1836 but the date of Figure 221 suggests that it was made later. An interesting example of how the potters selected, simplified and adapted their original source. This colour print was published by George Routledge and Sons in 1869.

honest it was more or less made for me. Even a moderately successful actor doesn't earn very much, it is well paid when you are working but sometimes the long wait between jobs can bring the yearly average down to a miserable level. Looking for work can be quite as hard as the work itself and of course when I should have been doing that I was working for nothing in the museums. It was when I discovered that people were willing to pay me for the knowledge I had acquired that I decided to make it my life instead of the theatre.

One thing I noticed with interest was that my long defended Staffordshire figures were not only returning to public favour but were at long last being appreciated for what they had always been, one of the richest schools of natural primitive art to have been discovered anywhere in the world. Over the years I had begun to notice them turning up more and more often on film and television sets or asserting themselves on the stages of West End theatres in anything from kitchen-sink dramas to plays set in the

223. The most rewarding part of research is to discover the identity of untitled portrait figures.
   Mr Palmer as the Earl of Warwick in King Henry VI part III, Act 4 Scene 3.
   "But Henry now shall wear the English Crown."
It pairs with Mr Holman as Faulconbridge in King John Act 3, Scene 2.
   "Austria's Head lie there."
Both prints originally published for Bell's British Library in 1786. The figures date c.1820. 7, 6½ ins.

elegant drawing rooms of the sophisticated rich. In any setting they looked equally attractive, which is part of their unique charm and explains why they now appeal to such a broad field of collectors. It was interesting to see that the set designers always chose to use figures of the Victorian period with their bold designs and clean, simple colours. Like all great primitive art they are bolder than life, they do not seek to photograph the human form like the earlier figures of Neale and the Woods or those of John and Rebecca Lloyd. Sherratt and Walton pointed the way and the Victorians in the youth and vigour of a new age found a new art to praise it.

As I travelled through England, always seeking and buying where I could, I had nothing to guide me except my own love and enthusiasm. Inevitably I made mistakes. With their new found popularity the first fakes and forgeries were beginning to appear and just as inevitably I was caught and bought some of them. (224, 225) Quite apart from those there were many genuine figures of inferior quality and I bought some of

Death of Nelson

Grace Darling

225. Another modern fake, this one turns up everywhere. *c.*1970. 6¼ ins.

224. A modern fake *c.*1970. Crude modelling, poor colour, heavily stained false crackle and stilted title. Some later efforts are better. 8½ ins.

those too. There is no sure and simple way for collectors to protect themselves, if we were all experts there would be no bargains and there are, thank goodness, still plenty of good figures to be bought at sensible prices.

When I first began collecting, many of the Victorian figures were sold at prices far below their true value but it would be very wrong to think that there are no more bargains to be found. Compared with other antiques and collectors' items of the nineteenth century, Staffordshire figures are still underpriced. It is true that some of them are being offered for sale at grossly inflated prices, sometimes because a dealer is being greedy but more often I suspect through ignorance. In either case the answer is simple. Shop around and compare prices until you find a dealer who is willing to help and advise you and whose expertise you can trust. A truly expert dealer should be able to date a figure very accurately to within a few years. He should be able in many cases to attribute it on stylistic evidence to a known factory or pot-bank, or at least be able to suggest from which of the six towns in the Staffordshire potteries a figure originated. He will know if an untitled figure is a portrait of a known personality and be able to quote the original source from which the potter worked. He will know if a figure has been repaired, restored or altered in any way and he will be happy to include all this

226. Three Generations. A superbly modelled figure by Thomas Parr. Queen
Victoria with the Prince of Wales and Princess Alexandra holding the baby
Duke of Clarence. Possibly modelled from an early photograph in the Royal
Archives at Windsor. *c.*1864. 9 ins. By courtesy of Mr and Mrs G. Barnett.

227. Henry V trying on the
Crown in the Jerusalem
Chamber, Westminster, in
March 1413 and very like Aunt
Liza preparing for Sunday
Chapel. The king was born at
Monmouth and I went to
school there so I like to picture
this on her mantel-shelf. Today
it is extremely rare. From a
print of a painting by John
Calcott Horsley. c.1847. 13¾ ins.

information on a proper signed receipt with a guarantee that all such facts are accurate
and that the figure itself is genuine. A collector should not be satisfied with less.

Antique fairs? Well, dealers will often save some of their best figures for them and it
can be pleasant to walk round and see what is on display, always remembering that
there are fairs and fairs. Grand antique fairs with a respected reputation will take
considerable trouble to see that all articles offered for sale are genuine and most dealers
exhibiting at them should be able to give a collector full and accurate receipts as
described above. You should also remember that they will have paid a great deal of
money to exhibit and that this must inevitably be reflected in their prices. To exhibit at
a top London antique fair today, in 1981, will often cost a dealer a minimum of £5,000
and usually considerably more.

In recent years antique fairs have become very popular but many of them are little
more than a glorified collection of junk. Don't despise them. When a collector has
acquired his own expertise they can be even more rewarding than expensive fairs and
there is always the exciting possibility of finding a rare figure tucked away among the
fakes and the modern reproductions. (224, 225)

Museums? There is no short cut to acquiring knowledge but enthusiasm will light up
the road and make it a pleasure. They are in a minority but some museums have good

228. During the First World War, Wilkinsons, the Royal Staffordshire Pottery, issued a set of eleven war leaders finely modelled by Carruthers Gould in a limited edition. King George V 1919. 11¾ ins. Marked, signed and dated.

229. For some reason Churchill was omitted from the 1914–18 set, possibly because he was blamed for the Dardenelles landings. Certainly eleven seems a curious number for a complete set. In 1941 Wilkinsons made amends and issued this handsome figure of The Former Naval Person in a limited edition, designed and signed by Clarice Cliff. 11¾ ins.

collections and you should see them if you can. I have made a list of the best at the end of this book. You won't be able to handle the exhibits but if you write and tell curators of your intended visit in advance you will always find your inquiries answered with kindness and courtesy. An expert dealer, too, will always be pleased to help you when you are starting and you will have the added advantage of being able to examine the figures yourself. I suppose it should be unnecessary to say it but it is best to try and choose a moment when he is not too busy – kinder anyway. If you write you should remember to enclose a stamped addressed envelope.

The bibliography on page 173 is not exhaustive. For the most part it contains only the books which helped me most when I was beginning, many of them have bibliographies of their own. Don't give up if they are out of print. Your local librarian will often be able to get a copy for you even if he doesn't have one himself. Our public library service is the best in the world and we should use it more than we do.

Sale-rooms? At the moment sale-rooms are getting rather bad publicity. Both dealers and the public complain that their charges are too high and that their conditions of sale are unfairly biased to their own advantage. A further complaint is made that the descriptions in their catalogues are often inaccurate and that in many cases no mention is made of repairs and restorations.

All this seems to me to be rather unfair. Sale-rooms are vast and efficient clearing houses for the quick and easy disposal of hundreds and thousands of lots almost every day of the week and it would be very strange if the occasional error didn't creep into their catalogues. As for their charges and conditions of sale, well, no one is forced to buy at auction and certainly no one can say that such charges and conditions are not clearly stated in every catalogue they publish.

If a collector knows his subject and if he has taken the trouble to view carefully before the sale, and it should be stressed that this precaution is advised by the sale-rooms themselves, then there is no reason why he should not buy with perfect safety.

Decide beforehand exactly how much you think the figure is worth to you and don't be tempted by sale-room fever to exceed that sum. This is the method invariably followed by experienced dealers and it makes sense. There is no point in bidding up against a reserve price which may have been over-optimistically insisted upon by an ambitious seller. It is the duty of the auctioneer to get the highest price he can for every lot in the sale, he would not be doing his job properly if he didn't. In the same way a bidder has a duty to himself to pay what he has decided is the true value to him as a collector and no more. A few over-enthusiastic nods can often double the selling price in a matter of seconds.

Some time ago I paid £1,680 at a London auction for a very rare figure of Sir Robert Peel seated proudly on the horse from which he was thrown and killed on June 29th, 1850. That was – and at the time of writing remains – a world record price for a Victorian Staffordshire figure at auction.

The figure was wrongly catalogued, being confused with a similar but cruder version of the same subject, but it made no difference, there were quite enough knowledgeable bidders in the sale-room who recognized it for what it was. This much rarer and finer version had been rumoured to exist for many years but it had never before appeared on the market. The interesting thing was not that the price was a world record but that for such a superbly potted figure of such great rarity it was so cheap. (Colour Plate VI) We bought it for stock and sold it within two days.

The sale made headline news on the art pages of newspapers all over the world with *The Times* and the *Daily Telegraph* devoting long articles to it. The real news for collectors is that so many other fine examples may still be bought for a small fraction of that world record price. A whole splendid parade of them, as fresh and colourful as the day they were made, waiting to brighten our shelves and to open a door to reveal the enchanted world of the primitive potters of Staffordshire, the Tribal Art of England.

Select Bibliography

Balston, Thomas. *Staffordshire Portrait Figures of the Victorian Age*. London 1958

Eaglestone, Arthur A. and Locket, Terence A. *The Rockingham Pottery* (new revised edition). Newton Abbot 1973

Earle, Cyril. *Earle Collection of Early Staffordshire Pottery*. London 1915

Falkner, Frank. *The Wood Family of Burslem*. London 1912

Godden, G. A. *British Pottery and Porcelain 1780–1850*. London 1963
   Encyclopaedia of British Pottery and Porcelain Marks. London 1964
   An Illustrated Encyclopaedia of British Pottery and Porcelain. London 1966

Haggar, Reginald G. *Staffordshire Chimney Ornaments*. London 1955

Jewitt, Llewellyn. *Ceramic Art of Great Britain* (2 vols). London 1878

Mountford, Arnold. *Staffordshire Salt-Glazed Stoneware*. London 1971

Oliver, Anthony. *The Victorian Staffordshire Figure*. London 1971

Owen, H. *The Staffordshire Potter*. London 1901

Pugh, P. D. G. *Staffordshire Portrait Figures and Allied Subjects of the Victorian Era*. London 1970

Read, Herbert. *Staffordshire Pottery Figures*. London 1929

Rice, D. G. *Rockingham Ornamental Porcelain*. London 1966

Rice, D. G. *An Illustrated Guide to Rockingham Pottery and Porcelain*. London 1971

Shaw, C. *(An Old Potter) When I was a Child*. London 1903

Shaw, Simeon. *History of the Staffordshire Potteries*. Hanley 1829

Shaw, Simeon. *The Chemistry used in the Manufacture of Porcelain Glass and Pottery*. Hanley 1837

Willett, Henry. *Catalogue of a Collection of Pottery and Porcelain Illustrating Popular British History lent by Henry Willett held at The Bethnal Green Branch of the Victoria and Albert Museum*. 1899 (The collection is now at Brighton Museum)

230. The shop in Kensington Church Street.

Museums

Museums and Exhibitions where good examples of Staffordshire Pottery may be seen by collectors

Brighton: The museum has some very fine pieces including the famous Willett Collection.

Cambridge: Fitzwilliam Museum. Some wonderful early pieces covering the eighteenth century including some stunning Pew Groups. They do have some good nineteenth century figures but it is wise to write first and ask when they may be seen.

London: British Museum. Mostly eighteenth and early nineteenth centuries. Salt-glazed stoneware. Pew Group. Astbury, Whieldon, Ralph Wood, some Walton and Sherratt.

Oliver-Sutton Antiques, 34 Kensington Church Street. Walton and Sherratt and the largest collection of nineteenth century Staffordshire figures in the world.

Victoria and Albert Museum. A really fine representative collection. Stronger on eighteenth century but some fair examples of the nineteenth century.

Melton Mowbray, Leicestershire. The Thomas Balston Collection is now part of the National Trust and is on view at Stapleford Park. Check opening days.

Stoke-on-Trent: City Museum and Art Gallery. A very impressive collection beautifully displayed. Not only very fine eighteenth century but they now have Admiral Pugh's nineteenth century collection of portrait figures.

Other museums which have some Staffordshire on display worth seeing are:

Leeds, Temple Newsum House
Manchester Museum and Art Gallery
Newcastle-under-Lyme Museum
Norwich Castle Museum
Nottingham Castle Museum
Wolverhampton Museum

Index